STUART O'GRADY
BATTLE SCARS

ACKNOWLEDGEMENTS

Thank you to everyone who made this book possible: to those interviewed, whether their names appear in these pages or not; to photographers, especially Graham Watson and Tim De Waele, and the family and friends – and fans – who have supported me in so many ways over the years.

STUART O'GRADY
BATTLE SCARS

WITH REECE HOMFRAY

hardie grant books
MELBOURNE · LONDON

An SBS Book

Published in 2014 by Hardie Grant Books

Hardie Grant Books (Australia)
Ground Floor, Building 1
658 Church Street
Richmond, Victoria 3121
www.hardiegrant.com.au

Hardie Grant Books (UK)
Dudley House, North Suite
34–35 Southampton Street
London WC2E 7HF
www.hardiegrant.co.uk

Cataloguing in publication data available from the National Library of Australia

Battle Scars

ISBN 9781742706399

Designed by Peter Daniel

Cover image © Richard Baybutt

Typeset in ITC New Baskerville Std 12/18.5pt

Printed and bound in Australia by Griffin Press

CONTENTS

INTRODUCTION

This book is about me and my bike. It's about an adventure that began thirty years ago and the emotional rollercoaster of life as a cyclist.

Cycling has been my obsession for almost my entire life and I've made more sacrifices than I can remember. I've ridden approximately 600,000 km, suffering on the roads day after day for over three decades. I've sacrificed being close to my family and friends. I've missed nearly every one of my family members' and friends' birthdays, weddings, funerals, and even the birth of my own daughter.

But what I have gained are experiences from riding my bike on almost every continent. I've been to more cities than I knew existed, met some of the most amazing people, been exposed to many different cultures and learnt new languages.

I've worn the green and gold for my country and I've sung our national anthem from the top step of the podium at an Olympic Games. I've ridden the Tour de France seventeen times and I've conquered the toughest one-day race that cycling can come up with in Paris–Roubaix.

But I've also broken almost every bone in my body several times over and made comebacks when doctors told me that my career could be well and truly over.

I met the woman of my dreams who has been with me for the best and also the toughest moments of my life. Anne-Marie has been my rock and the foundation of my career, bringing up our beautiful family on the other side of the world, far from her own family and friends. She has done it just as tough as I have and never complained—well, maybe once. Anne-Marie can tell you that professional cycling is not all about podiums, flowers and champagne even though that's how we met. It's a tough job and only the strongest make it through the other end.

These are the parts of my life that I wouldn't change for the world. But I've also done things that I wish I could change and made decisions that I am not proud of. Life is a challenge and as human beings, we tend to make mistakes and bad judgements and I am no different from anyone else.

My life was good in 1998. I was young, healthy and doing what I loved. But for some reason—maybe deep down I was scared of failure or of letting people down—I was not strong enough to resist the pressure and temptation to go down a path that I openly swore I would never follow: doping.

It may have been only a tiny moment in my career, but the person I cheated the most was myself, and that feeling of guilt will haunt me forever. I have to live with that. But I can also still hold my head high due to everything I achieved throughout my career while racing clean, and this means the world to me.

My family also means the world to me; they are the sole focus of my life. I can now give back to them the care and support they've given me for the past twenty-three years. From here on, it's no longer about me. It's about guiding and helping others through their own adventure so they make the right decisions, whether it be in cycling or in life.

All I ever wanted to do was make my family and friends proud. And to everyone who has been there for me through the good and the bad—made a phone call, sent a text message, an email or a letter—I say a massive thank you. You've all played a part in making this one amazing life cycle.

STUEY, DECEMBER 2013

CHAPTER 1

BORN TO RIDE

Veteran cycling coach and manager Shayne Bannan remembers
the first day he met Stuart O'Grady. 'The AIS group was doing
efforts up Norton Summit, and it was a pretty talented group,
when this little red-headed kid turned up and started following
us up,' Bannan recalls.

'I looked around and thought, "Shit, this little fellow is still
there." He was still there when we got to the top, so I went over
and said, "G'day mate, what's your name?" And this quiet little
voice says, "Stuart … Stuart O'Grady." Then I asked him how
old he was, and he replied that he was fourteen. "Oh, you'll
make a good little bike-rider one day," I told him.

The competitive little engine inside me has always been there, and as a kid I fuelled it with both my love of bike-riding and the hard work that went with it. I had a daily ritual that even seasoned professionals would have been proud of. From the age of thirteen when I was unleashed—finally allowed to ride my bike on my own—my routine was always the same: wake up in the morning, record the time, my heart-rate, the weather and how I was feeling in a diary. Go to school. Get home from school, eat a sandwich, grab my bike, hit the start button on the stopwatch on my way out of the driveway and go full gas. I had mapped out my own 30 km time-trial course and every day was a chance to go faster than the day before. The carefully planned route started at my family home at Ingle Farm, went up Tea Tree Gully and Range Road, down Anstey's Hill, along Lower North East Road and back home. The more times I did it, the more serious I got. Even if it was pouring with rain, I'd still be out there, sitting at the traffic lights fuming that I was losing valuable time.

When I finished my ride I'd go back to my diary and write my maximum speed, my total time, how I was feeling and what time I went to bed. Dad has always been big on keeping a diary so I probably got that from him because I kept it up for years afterwards.

This was my diary entry from 28 November 1991. I was eighteen years old and my training had obviously pro-gressed a fair bit from time-trialling after school:

Woke up at 6.45 am. Got dressed, had breakfast. Came outside and did rollers 15 km in 27 mins. Got changed, rode up to the corner and met bunch. Up the Gorge, along to Birdwood, then Mt Torrens, right turn to Lobethal from downhill, attacked all the way through the Gorge. Absolutely stomping, five of us left. Down Lwr Nth East Rd, Portrush Rd, Henk and I went thru city to home. Had lunch, had 5 x 15 min ergo sessions. Mega hard. Knackered after. Shower, stretching, had tea, watched TV, cleaned bike. Bed, new quilt.

Morn HR—37
Dist—120 km
Time—4 hrs
Ave—30 km/h
Mxs—78 km/h
Felt—Pretty good, tired after ergo
Weather—Fine and warm, perfect 24 degrees
Bed—10 pm

Even as a teenager, my life revolved around cycling. As for who was directly responsible for my cycling genes—I got hit from both sides thanks to my mum, Fay, and dad, Brian. Dad was a really strong rider who was second in the state championships a couple of times and a real hard-nut. He won the Kangaroo Island Tour twice and in 1971 won a 200-lap points race at Hanson Reserve, which back then was the biggest points race in South Australia.

There were four children in Mum's family and they all had a go at cycling at some stage. My uncle Bob Baird was the best rider, going to the 1964 Tokyo Olympics where he was fourth in the team pursuit, and his older brother Lyle was a very strong state-level rider. So with Dad's hard-nut gene and my uncles' speed and power, I got the right mix.

Ingle Farm, where I grew up, is about 15 km from Adelaide and nestled in the working-class northern suburbs where my parents still live to this day. Dad was a panel-beater working for the government and Mum worked in aged care when she wasn't flat out running us kids around. My brother, Darren, was the eldest, followed by me, then our sister, Lesley, at four-year intervals.

Mum and Dad didn't have a lot of money but they were so supportive and wanted to give us the best education they could. I went to two private schools, St Gabriel's and St Paul's College. We were aware of the sacrifices Mum and Dad made for us to have private schooling so there was no place for misbehaving. On weekends they'd take us to play just about every sport possible. It wasn't unusual for me to go from soccer in the morning to quickly getting changed in the car and being taken to a bike race in the afternoon. But not once in my entire life can I say that Dad ever told me to go for a ride. Perhaps, had he pushed me into cycling, I mightn't have gone on with it because I've seen what pushy parenting does to kids and it isn't good.

Still, I was surrounded by cycling growing up. I've got early memories of being around Hanson Reserve Velodrome in Adelaide's western suburbs watching Dad race. We were just kids running around under the lights, not taking much notice of the racing on the outdoor bitumen track with dodgy chicken-wire fencing. But, as with anything your dad does, you want to copy. I wanted to be a panel-beater until I realised there was such a thing as professional cycling.

From an early age Dad would take me on rides. He made a seat on the top tube of his bike and I'd try to hang on as we went through the back streets of Ingle Farm. The seat was not much bigger than a passport and made of plywood covered with foam but I thought it was brilliant.

It was the freedom that got me with cycling. To be able to go anywhere, anytime. I'd stand in the driveway and watch Dad and Darren disappear on their bikes into the distance, then wait for them to come home. They'd finally get back, after what seemed like hours, and I'd say, 'Where have you guys been?' and they'd say, 'Oh, the beaches and the hills' and I was like, 'Man I want to do that!'. The best I could wrangle was being allowed to ride around the block or to a mate's house.

My first real bike was a solid steel, metallic red Elizabeth Star that weighed about 15 kilograms—a far cry from the lightweight carbon machines they race on now. Dad reckons it was the heaviest bike the world had ever seen, but to me it was my dream machine. Before that, I had BMXs but this was my first road bike. It was Christmas morning and I'd been begging for a bike. I clearly remember going into Mum and Dad's bedroom and pulling back the curtains but just seeing a set of wheels on the floor. I was devastated. I couldn't believe they'd just got me the wheels! Then I opened the other curtain and there was

9

the frame. You know those kids you see riding through the streets with a grin from ear to ear on Christmas morning? I was one of them.

When summer holidays were over I rode it to school every day. I wasn't an A-grade student by any means but I never copped a detention because that would have meant missing out on riding my bike. I played a lot of soccer and cricket but athletics and cycling soon took over and eventually I had to choose. Surprisingly, it was really easy because while I was good at running and finished second in the state cross country championships, I hated it. You could run for 40 minutes and would only get around the block which was fairly boring. Dad actually tried to hold me back from racing my bike until I was fifteen, which was when Darren started, but I cracked it and managed to convince him to bring it forward to thirteen.

My first race was at Regency Park, a 30-minute criterium on a Sunday morning around an industrial block in Adelaide's inner-north. I attacked like crazy from the start and got away with a girl and when we got the bell lap I saw her go for the drink bottle so I attacked with everything I had. Unfortunately she caught me and won the race. Later on I had people telling me that what I did was pretty sneaky, but all I saw was an opportunity so I grabbed it.

It took me a long time to win a race because I was a pretty small kid. I had no sprint so all I could do was attack and hope for the best. But eventually I started winning and copped severe handicaps like being put a lap behind so I'd have to attack, catch up a whole lap and do it again. We'd get $2 prize-money for winning a race, which was pretty high stakes in those days. If we cleaned up, my friend and I would go straight to the fish and chip shop; two bucks would get you a kilo of hot chips. Then we'd go riding for the rest of the day.

When I wasn't racing on weekends my mates and I would ride all day—we'd be gone for six or seven hours and some days we'd sprint to every single bus stop on the roadside just to test each other out. My after-school rides also got longer as I discovered the Adelaide Hills and often I wouldn't get home until dark, causing Mum plenty of angst.

'One evening after school while Brian was still at work I got a call,' remembers Fay. "Mum, I've broken down, I've used all my spare tubes and I'm at Kersbrook." I was worried sick.

'So I'm panicking and it's a fair drive out to Kersbrook [26 km through the hills]. When I finally got there, the first thing I noticed was a ute and Stu's bike lying on the road next to it. Then I recognised it was my brother-in-law's ute. He lived at Springton and luckily just happened to be going through town when he saw Stu at the phone box.'

The other moment that is still inked in Fay's memory is taking a phone call and hearing that Stuart had been riding his bike to school one morning and had collided with a motorbike. 'He hit a man-hole cover and because it was raining the roads were wet and he slid across the road into the path of an oncoming motorbike,' Fay said.

'Stuart was okay, a bit frightened, and his bike was okay, the front wheel just had to be re-built, but the motorbike had $800 worth of damage. Thank God we had that on our insurance policy.'

The rain wouldn't stop us from riding; we'd stick bread-bags over our shoes and tie them with a rubber band to make instant waterproof shoe-covers. As a kid, if I wasn't out riding there was a good chance I was at a bloke named Pud Brooks' house in Pennington. Pud was a Port Adelaide Cycling Club legend who built bikes in his back shed. I'd help him out and he'd repay me with a pair of brake pads or handlebar tape, and I'd listen to him tell his stories and watch him build anything to do with a bike.

Even though we lived in the northern suburbs, I always rode for Port Adelaide Cycling Club because it was Dad's club—not that it helped me when I was trying to get the final spot on the state juvenile team to ride the team pursuit and Dad was the coach. There were two of us trying out for the last spot on the team and one of the kids wasn't Dad's son. We did our test and were pretty even but Dad came up and said, 'I can't put you in, mate. I've got to put the other kid in because it would look bad.' I was pretty pissed off but Dad wouldn't budge on it. My own dad left me out of the state team! I couldn't believe it. In hindsight, though, he probably did me a favour because it threw a heap of fuel on the fire and made me even more determined. I was like, 'Right, you're not ever going to have to worry about not picking me again.'

I eventually did crack the South Australian team and my first interstate trip was to Canberra when I was fifteen. I was sixth in a bunch sprint at the National Road Championships, and not being a sprinter, I realised there might be some potential there. My first time on the track didn't go so well. I nearly ended up over the handlebars because I forgot about the fixed gear and stopped pedalling—but you learn that pretty quickly. I also learnt that it was a big deal to ride for SASI—the South Australian Sports Institute—and I was massively envious of those riders. They had SASI kits and team bikes, which was the ultimate for me at that age.

After racing at Hanson Reserve one day, Mick Turtur, the SASI coach, came over to the middle of the track and said, 'Mate, do you want to get on board?' By then I was sixteen and it was like I'd just been offered a spot on the Olympic team. In an instant I had a coach, training times, access to the facilities and felt like a real cyclist.

Turtur, a 1984 Olympic gold medallist, reflects on Hanson Reserve's glory years as 'the good old days'. He says Stuart was a 'scrawny, skinny kid who would have weighed 50 kg wringing wet' but showed unbelievable potential.

'He was fourteen or fifteen and a complete standout. You could see very clearly that he had something special from the way he applied himself on the bike. He had ability beyond his years and it was coupled with a fierce determination and desire,' Turtur says.

'He showed style in the way he rode, he was very intelligent in that he could read a race and he had all the physiological attributes.'

One of Turtur's fondest memories from that era was partnering with Stuart for the Australian Teams Challenge—a two-man omnium event at Hanson Reserve in 1990. Stuart was seventeen and still at school while Turtur was thirty-two with an Olympic gold medal.

'I said to him, "I bet I can get more points than you,"' Turtur recalls. 'Which I eventually did but I had to ride my absolute arse off, I had to lay it all down. Stuart is one of the toughest, hardest competitors I have ever seen in my life—in any sport. What he's put himself through, some of the crashes he's had— the majority of people would never come back from.'

Training with the state team meant the occasional training ride with the national team which was pretty cool. I would tag along with guys like Brett Aitken, Steve McGlede, Shaun O'Brien and Mark Kingsland. Often our training rides would head up the Gorge and I'd be hanging in there for dear life. A lot of them would comment, 'You're going alright for a little freckly kid.' I was desperate to impress the older guys, which meant a lot of suffering trying to keep up with them.

The main person I was trying to impress was the national coach, Charlie Walsh. Charlie was an intimidating man. For starters, he rode with us every day and was a man of few words, but they were hard words. If you started climbing and moving your head he'd be barking at you, or if you weren't pedalling smoothly he'd be yelling at you not to rock. But he also gave credit where it was due which meant a lot of encouragement for me to keep going.

Walsh, a legendary cycling coach who oversaw a golden era for the sport in Australia in the 1980s and 1990s, recalls Stuart turning up to Norton Summit in Adelaide's east as a fourteen-year-old while the senior squad was training.

'I didn't mind him joining in and already he was competitive,' Walsh said. 'I had a very strong belief that Stuart would go a long way. Before I even had him in the program I said, "If ever I've seen anybody, this kid will ride the Tour de France."

'And when he came to us as a seventeen-year-old you could see the quality of him. He was fiercely competitive, very smart and aggressive—all the qualities you would look for in a cyclist.'

STUART O'GRADY

'When he came into the program, my first instructions were, "I want to gradually feed you in." He was a little reluctant to accept this because he wanted to be crashing in. If the seniors were doing 250 km, I started him off at 180 km to 200 km which is still a fair amount. He stuck with this but within two months he was up doing what the others were doing—but he wanted to do it as well or better than them.'

Walsh said he wasn't worried about Stuart being such a small kid training for an event that required such enormous power through the pedals. 'What he could deliver was top-shelf,' Walsh said.

Twenty years later Walsh was asked where he rated Stuart among every athlete he had ever worked with. Walsh said his decision was based on four benchmarks—physical attributes, psychology, leadership and personality in terms of respecting people around them.

'I rate Stuart top in all of those qualities,' said Walsh, who has photos of Stuart and his signed yellow jersey on the walls of his Adelaide home. 'Any coach, if they had an athlete like Stuart O'Grady, they'd walk around smiling every day.'

At 7.5 km long and averaging 4.1 per cent gradient, Norton Summit remains a popular climb for cyclists in Adelaide. At the top is a well-known pub, the Scenic Hotel, where hanging on the wall are three jerseys including one yellow and one green from the Tour de France, personally signed by Stuart. Little did Stuart know as a teenager, grinding his way past the hotel sometimes five times per session, that it would one day house the two most famous cycling jerseys in the world—both with his name on them.

Cycling was slowly becoming my life and everything I did, from stretching in the mornings to eating the right foods and training the right way, had a purpose. I was literally living and breathing cycling. I'd buy bike magazines and when I wasn't riding my bike I'd be cleaning it or tinkering with it.

Slowly I started learning about the world of European cycling. My first 'Euro' experience was watching an old VHS video in, of all things, Dutch. Adelaide cyclist Pat Jonker and his dad Evert, who were very supportive of me and good friends, gave me a video of the 1984 Paris–Roubaix. I didn't have a clue what the commentators were saying but you could hear the excitement in their voices. Guys were covered in mud and were crashing everywhere. I was gobsmacked as Irishman Sean Kelly rode to victory. While most teenage boys I knew dreamt of kicking the winning goal in a football grand final or playing Test cricket for Australia, I wanted nothing more than to become a professional cyclist.

If I was going to be a proper bike-rider, I figured I better start shaving my legs. The first time was a disaster. I was that embarrassed that I locked myself in the bathroom and ripped my legs to shreds with an old cheap and nasty blade. Everyone noticed it and gave me heaps of shit but I said, 'I'm a bike-rider and if I crash or get a massage ... you know.' (Not that I was even getting massages at that point but I had all the excuses ready to go and had my whole life planned).

One day at school we were asked to write down what we wanted to be when we grew up. My plan was to get an electrical apprenticeship. I hoped it would lead to becoming a fireman because then I could have four days on and four days off to train, which would allow me to become a pro cyclist. Everyone laughed it off because I don't think there'd been more than three Australian professionals in the history of the sport—Neil Stephens, Stephen Hodge and Phil Anderson—but they were the three names I wrote on my pencil case at school.

I wanted to get my plan moving along quickly so after Year 11, I enrolled in TAFE to do my electrical engineering course which would advance me to a second-year apprenticeship and a job. Cycling was still my priority though. I'd be up at 5 am, lights on the bike, and do 60 km on my race bike with my backpack full of books, shoes and clothes. Then I'd stop at my nanna's house, get my old crappy bike that purposely had no handlebar tape and only one brake so no one would steal it, and off I'd go to TAFE. Afterwards it was back to Nanna's, eat a quick sandwich, swap the bikes and set out to do 100 km. I had the same loop along the beach to Port Adelaide, Outer Harbour, Glenelg, Anzac

Highway, Cross Road, the foothills and back to Ingle Farm, finishing in the dark every night. No one ever told me to do it but in my mind that's what I needed to do. I'd get home, have dinner, study and go to bed. I guess it wasn't much fun in the winter but I don't have any horror stories. I never came off my bike or anything like that—I must have been saving it all for later.

Things started to get serious after I won two gold medals at my first junior national titles—the 30 km points race and 4 km team pursuit—because that got me on the Australian team for the 1990 junior world championships. I was only a first-year junior (sixteen years old) which was a pretty massive thing for me. I got the green and gold shirts and Mum sewed the badges on for me, then we had to come up with the money to go overseas because the junior world championships were being held in Middlesbrough in the UK. I had a newspaper round and did odd-jobs, and Port Adelaide Cycling Club held barbecues and raffles that really helped me get the money together. I was the first one from our family to go overseas so they were pretty exciting times; by comparison, the whole TAFE electrical thing was suddenly looking fairly average.

Before the junior worlds we had a training camp in Italy with the national coach, Nino Solari. He took us to a road race in Rieti and we were thrown in. We rocked up to see all these Bianchi team cars, kids with all the same bikes and fully kitted out—it was like watching Real Madrid or Barcelona FC run out. We were there in shabby tracksuits, our bikes weren't matching and we'd come rolling along in a little blue mini-van. I felt so out of place and thought, 'These guys are going to kill us.' But funnily enough, I ended up winning the race. Guys were attacking and as we got to the climb, I did a little acceleration and all of a sudden I was solo and rode to the finish line. I was in disbelief because for an Australian junior to win over there caused quite a stir. I started thinking that this road racing business was pretty cool, but still my focus was on track racing and my dream was to race for Australia on the boards at an Olympic Games. Our junior team won a bronze medal in the team pursuit at the worlds and I did the points race and road race but was nothing special. My first junior world championship teammates were Tim O'Shannessy, who I still keep in contact with; James Cross; Matthew Gilmore, who's a national coach for the Australian track team; and Damian McDonald.

Tragically, Damian was killed in 2007 in an accident in Melbourne's Burnley Tunnel. I have so many fond memories of us going through the junior program and we rode together until 1996. Damien was a really funny guy, the comedian of the group, and a great bloke. I was pretty shocked when I heard about the accident; he had a young child at the time and it was very sad.

After my first junior worlds experience, I reluctantly dragged myself back to TAFE where my teachers told me I was so far behind that I would have to cram to get the certificate. So, like my cycling training, I threw everything at it, did the work and got it done. This led to an apprenticeship in 1990 working at the Royal Australian Air Force Base at Edinburgh, about 20 km north of Adelaide. I gave my first pay-cheque to Mum and Dad because that was apparently what you were meant to do in those days. Besides, I owed them everything anyway.

I liked the job because it fitted into my plan. I'd ride to work every day, sometimes in the rain, and my workmates would say, 'Where have you ridden from, Ingle Farm?' They thought I was crazy.

Three months into the job everything was going great. Just as I'd been given all my tools, my toolbox and clothing, I got a phone call from Charlie Walsh asking me to come and see him. Dad came with me because I wasn't old enough to drive myself. Charlie was the big dog of Australian cycling but because I'd seen him at training from time to time, I wasn't nervous. I knew it couldn't be a bad thing because I hadn't been in trouble. All I could think about was Charlie inviting me into the Australian Institute of Sport. And he did. But it was what came next that really shocked me. I didn't have time for the first bit of news to sink in before he said, 'I'd also like you to have a crack at the Olympics.' Here I was, a seventeen-year-old apprentice electrician living at home with Mum and Dad, and Charlie Walsh wanted me to train for the 1992 Barcelona Olympics!

Don't get me wrong. I was dreaming of the Olympics, but of 1996—not in two years' time! As we left, Charlie told me to have a think about it. When we got home I expected Dad to say, 'Look, you're seventeen, realistically you're probably not going to make the Olympic team and you've just got an apprenticeship so let's just leave it.' But he said the exact opposite: 'Why not? Go for it, you can always come back and finish your apprenticeship.' It was as though God had uttered the words I'd been waiting for my whole life. I've still got the diary entry from that day on 8 April 1991:

> *BIGGEST DAY OF MY LIFE. Woke at 6.30 am, got ready to go to work. Waited for David, didn't come. Dad had to take me on m/bike, got a bench job because of foot—sore as. Andy gave me a lift home, got so sore went to doctors, bandaged up, antibiotics. Went to Charlie's; one of the biggest decisions I've ever made. Joining the AIS—quit work ASAP. Olympics here I come. I WANT IT NOW. Not going to work tomorrow.*

Luckily for me, the national program was in Adelaide so I could still live at home. All the other guys lived together in a house and they did it tough with no family, no mates and the house was a disaster. They were all in their mid-twenties and I was the new kid. I knew Brett Aitken, who was a bit of an idol for me, and they were all pretty cool and accepting of me.

22

Aitken was two years older than Stuart when the younger boy first caught his eye at the 1990 national track titles where, as a bottom-age junior, he won the points race in commanding style. By the time he officially joined the national squad, Aitken said Stuart was already 'a force to be reckoned with'.

'He was just a scrawny little kid, he weighed next to nothing and was a late bloomer,' Aitken says. 'But when he came out training with us he was almost impossible to shake off. You quite often get a kid who is good in one area but Stuey could do anything on the track and he was fearless.'

Stuart's brother, Darren, left home to join the army at the age of seventeen and said he missed the five crucial years in which his little brother went from talented teenager to a beast on two wheels.

'When I left home Stuart was a little kid and when I came back he was nineteen and tearing up the track,' Darren says. 'I was allowed to go on their training rides up Norton Summit and in those days they'd do it ten times, on the drops, in the saddle, flat out every time. I'd take that training to my mountain biking and it was very motivational, to put it mildly.'

2
3

 Darren remembers standing at a stage finish of the Tour Down Under in Adelaide one year looking at an antique photographic display. It turned out the husband of the lady running the display was Stuart's old boss when he was an electrical apprentice. 'He was the guy who suggested to Stuart he probably wasn't making a good decision to go bike-riding full-time,' Darren says.

'And I know what our parents were like when I was growing up. Bike-riding was a hobby at best, and it was a dangerous hobby and relatively expensive. So for Stuey to give up a career for cycling was massive. It's a fairytale, especially for a sports person in Australia. It was a major, major gamble and that's why Stuey has put in the hard yards and made sure the gamble paid off.'

If I thought 100 km after TAFE every day was enough to prepare me for the training that would follow, I was mistaken. I've still got the training programs from Charlie at home and they would blow you away. Every single session for the entire year was mapped out. Most days I'd meet the boys at Holden Hill near the police station; I couldn't afford to be one minute late because these guys were coming up as a group and weren't waiting. A few times I'd see them coming and if they got the green traffic light I'd have to chase just to start training; it was insane. I've never trained that hard even as a professional. The workload was unbelievable—you're talking 120 km, 160 km, 180 km, 220 km, 260 km days then a day off consisting of 60 km. The next day, 220 km then 240 km with the odd 280 km thrown in for good measure to really put us on our hands and knees. We'd go through Victor Harbor, the Barossa and Gawler—where the Tour Down Under goes through these days—and it broke a lot of blokes. But I thrived on it. I saw those big days as a massive challenge and I used to love it. I'd think, 'How far can I actually go?'

One day we had 280 km on the program but I did another 20 km just to get 300 km on the speedo. I got home at 6 pm completely crossed up ten hours later. But Charlie had to turn this boy into a man in eighteen months before the Barcelona Olympics. I knew he was giving me a hard time but I was on the Olympic squad; I was like, 'Come on, give it to me.'

But training only got easier after that. Okay, the racing was in another world but I never trained that hard again and Charlie made me what I am. If I had the engine, Charlie fine-tuned it, and if I was ever going to crack and throw it in, it would have been then. Thankfully, I didn't.

CHAPTER 2

NO PAIN
NO GAIN

Even though I'd been called into the AIS with Charlie and the boys, I still rode the junior world championships in Colorado Springs in 1991. I did the individual pursuit, team pursuit and finished the points race after a rain delay on the Sunday night. The very next morning I was back with Charlie who was in Colorado on an altitude camp preparing for the senior world titles. That first morning Charlie had us doing 5 x 5 km efforts and I had to pack it in after a couple. It was the only time I'd ever not finished a session, and it happened to be my first day on the senior team. But the next day I was back on the full program and desperate to show the guys I could hang in there. We were also doing 200 km rides at altitude which was an eye-opener, but again

I managed to hang in and suffer through with them.

Things didn't get much easier when we went to our base camp in Buttgen, Germany, where we were on a super-steep indoor wooden velodrome. All of a sudden we had the pursuit bars and double disc wheels and the first effort we did was absolute lightning. I did a turn, swung up the track and had never been that fast when I came back down on the aero bars and missed Brett Aitken's rear wheel by a centimetre. 'Holy shit,' I thought, 'that must have looked good.'

At the junior worlds we won the bronze medal in the team pursuit in 4:24 and when we rocked up for the senior world championships in Stuttgart, Charlie had me starting which is probably the hardest position out of the four because you start, get the team wound up to max speed then swing up three-quarters of a lap later. Charlie had us running to a 4:10 schedule—which is a whole lap quicker than I'd gone two weeks before. I thought, 'You have got to be kidding'—fourteen seconds faster than I'd ever been in my life, my first senior world titles and I was starting. I was shitting myself but the nerves must have helped because we ended up breaking the record with a 4:10—me, Brett Aitken, O'Brien and McGlede.

Back then it was fast, nowadays we'd get our arses kicked, but when you have a fast, controlled team it runs smoothly. It hurts more when you're going full gas and the pace keeps dropping off. Unfortunately the Germans came out a few minutes later and went quicker again, but for me to go from one extreme to another in such a short period was pretty amazing.

After the rush of my first senior world championships we had a month off, which was most welcome. But it was only a matter of time before Charlie called us up and gave us a training program that set out what we'd be doing every single day for the whole year—from what time breakfast would be, to when we would stretch. We were booked to do some 300 km rides and it was pretty scary to contemplate. But every training session was a day closer to my dream of riding at the Barcelona Olympics. There were only five of us in the endurance team so it was already looking like a real possibility.

In January 1992, we went to Mexico for a training camp and the volume of training was out of control. When I look back and remember we were training for a four-minute event and clocking up 800 to 1000 km a week, it was pretty hardcore. We'd go on ten-hour rides through Mexico and be scattered all over the countryside because I would treat it like a race. I wanted to push not only myself, but the other boys to chase me, all day if they had to. The boys must've hated me. I'd get back to the hotel, rest for an hour before my roommate would get home and throw his shoes across the room, hating life. But the next day we'd do it all again.

Australian cycling journalist Rupert Guinness, who covered Stuart's entire career, remembers a training camp in Toluca, Mexico, in the build-up to the 1996 Atlanta Olympics when he watched Stuart ride away from his teammates, just as Walsh predicted.

'Walsh pitted his charges over a 295 km training ride including several mountains over which they had to ride in their biggest and hardest gear and up to an altitude that would edge closer to 4000 metres,' Guinness says.

'Following in the team van, Walsh warned that it would be the last time we'd see O'Grady for the day. He went as far as to say we would catch him at the hotel. I laughed, thinking he might be exaggerating. He wasn't.

'By the time everyone got back to the hotel O'Grady was showered, dressed in casual gear, smiling, and there to take bikes off his exhausted teammates as they dismounted. I knew O'Grady had a massive engine but that astonished me for someone who was still twenty-three.'

I loved the challenge Charlie would throw at me because I knew he was testing me; he was pushing me to the limit. Some days he'd stand on the inside of the track and hold up two fingers which meant I had to do a two-lap turn, then the next day he'd test me again and hold up three fingers. It hurt like hell but I thrived on it.

After the Mexico camp we were measured up for our suits which meant we were going to the Olympics. But we still didn't know who was going to ride when we got there.

I remember being excited but not as overwhelmed or emotional as I thought I would be. Probably because I knew what still lay ahead of us. We went back to Germany for a few weeks before the Games and every single session I gave 100 per cent. There was no way I was going to let my opportunity slip. The training really pushed me to the limit; for example, we would do a day like this:

5.30 am – 30 mins rollers

6.15 am – stretching

7.30 am – breakfast

8.45 am – 30 min warm-up on track

9.30 am – 10 x 4 km teams pursuits (each one faster and faster until the last one was full gas) 15min warm down

12.30 pm – lunch

2 pm – 30 min warm-up on track

2.45 pm – 10 x 2 km teams pursuits (flying start and again last effort would be 100% or approx 1.56 min)

5pm to 6pm – 30 km road ride

7 pm – dinner

The Olympics finally arrived in July. I'll never forget walking into the athletes' village for the first time. Here I was, eighteen, surrounded by hundreds of the best athletes on the planet in the biggest sporting event on earth; I had to pinch myself, I was that awestruck. The Olympics is as big as it gets, it's the ultimate for any athlete. There are guys who are seven-foot tall, girls who are 140 kg weightlifters, and every single person is at the top of their game.

First up in qualifying, bang: an Olympic record of 4:11. We were the fastest qualifiers which meant that for the first time we'd gone quicker than Germany. It gave us a massive boost but also meant a lot of nerves because I think we realised that suddenly anything was possible. Second round, bang: fastest again and we were into the Olympic final the following night. I remember Shayne Bannan, who was assistant coach to Charlie at the time, telling me when I was young that a true professional athlete can switch off at night and go to sleep. But I was never able to do that my whole career. I would get into bed and start analysing everything: what if this happens, what if that happens?

I was absolutely crapping myself on the start line for the final, my hands and arms were shaking. During moments like that you feel like you're having an out-of-body experience. You take off and it's so loud in the velodrome, people are screaming, but you don't hear them because the screams all intertwine into one huge ball of noise. You're just focused on your breathing and you're that paranoid about making a stupid mistake like clipping a wheel that you forget where you are. You drill yourself with thousands of kilometres of practice that by the time you take off, it's serenity.

When the race started I couldn't wait to get to the front and rip it up. One of the boys was struggling a bit, the pace was dropping off and I was frustrated because I knew we weren't going fast enough. In a pursuit on the track the coach will walk a line to indicate to the riders whether they are up or down on their schedule.

That night, Charlie started walking the wrong way and I was getting angrier and angrier. We ended up losing the final to Germany by 1.5 seconds after they rode 4:08.7 and we clocked 4:10.2. You'd think that at eighteen years of age and in my first Olympics I'd be happy, but I reckon I was the angriest I'd ever been in my entire life. In photos of that moment, I don't have a smile in any of them because watching the Germans on the podium with their gold medal, I was spewing. I knew we were going quicker, we all knew we could have done better, and this was an Olympic Games. I thought I might never get that opportunity again.

Brett Aitken says the pain on Stuart's face was obvious by the tears rolling down his cheeks as they stood in the middle of the velodrome listening to the German national anthem. 'It wasn't an indication of any weakness but of how much it meant to him.'

After a few hours when the adrenaline had gone we went out. We were one of the first events in the Olympics so had quite a bit of time to have some fun. This partying mindset continued when I got home and for the first time I lived the life of an eighteen-year-old and went pretty crazy for a few weeks. I definitely didn't want to go riding for a while, which was pretty normal. When Charlie called us up for the next round of testing and training it was a fair wake-up call and there was no easing into it—Norton Summit four times a day. The new season rolled around and by the start of 1993 we'd lost McGlede and O'Brien and our team became a whole lot younger. I later found out that Charlie had made a bet that our team pursuit wouldn't even make the top eight at the world championships. Aside from me we had Brett, O'Shannessy and Billy-Joe Shearsby who came into the program that year; we had no idea what to expect. But it was a good group of guys, a mix of personalities. We trained hard and, amazingly, we ended up winning the world championship in world-record time. Not a bad turnaround from what was first expected of us. With a new team I had to step up a bit and it all started in training. I was so competitive; every time we went up Norton Summit I had to be first, or every effort we did I had to do the longest turn; I was always pushing it.

34

We'd barely raced together when we went to the world titles in Norway and had no idea what was going to happen. What did happen shocked us. The first ride was a world record 4:07 and Charlie made us stay up until 1 am when drug control came over to confirm the world record. I remember sitting there saying, 'Mate, I haven't even hit third gear yet, we're going to go quicker tomorrow, I can guarantee it.'

We rocked up and absolutely obliterated it with a 4:03 to beat Germany in the final. I started and did a two-lap turn and kept it up the whole race. A 4:03 back then was unheard of, it was ridiculous, but Charlie had done his job perfectly. It was the first time Australia had won the team pursuit world championship. Coming in as such big underdogs and going that quick, then standing in the rainbow jersey—it was pretty special.

Walsh and Aitken say that the 1993 world championship campaign is one of their most enduring memories of Stuart.

'I started the year with four cyclists—that's all, no spares, no nothing,' Walsh says. 'Stuart was an outstanding leader in the way he trained and the way he backed in and supported the coach. Whatever I asked, he did it with all the ferocity he could muster.'

Walsh explains that the general rules of a four-man team pursuit is that each rider does one lap on the front, then swings high up the track, waits for the team to come past then backs down at the end of the line repeatedly for 4 km.

'Now and again a country will have a bloke who can do a two-lap turn and they're superheroes,' he says. 'So I started the year with four riders and said to them, "When we go to the world championships, each of you will be capable of doing two-lap turns." I knew Stuart and Brett were capable of that already.

'Then one day when we were training in Germany, Stuart came up to me and said, "Charlie, do you have a restriction on two-lap turns?"

'I said, "No, I don't, and in fact I'd encourage you to do it and failure is not a concern. I don't mind if people want to challenge themselves and if you fail there's no consequences."

'So the next day we're out on the training track and Stuart starts ripping in three-lap turns, then he got up to four-lap turns—at a phenomenal pace.

'Now that is huge leadership to the group—"Here am I, challenging myself." So Brett Aitken takes on the challenge, and the two others take it on. You could see the psychology of the leadership and it was all for the team.'

Aitken says Stuart's multiple-lap turns were an 'integral part' of the team 'smashing' the world record. 'That [two-lap turns] was basically unheard of back then.'

It was still all about the track until 1994 when we went to Italy for the world championships. One afternoon after training I was hanging out with the boys in the middle of the track when an Italian guy came over and said he wanted to chat to me about turning professional on the road. It caught me completely by surprise because I hadn't even considered such a thing. But he said he knew the manager of the Polti team and they were interested in me.

The next day I got a phone call from Chris Board-man's manager who said he was downstairs at the hotel and wanted to talk. At that point, Boardman was Olympic champion in the individual pursuit and one of my idols so I couldn't get to the meeting quick enough. He asked me if I was interested in joining the GAN team—a French team—of which Boardman was the only English-speaking rider. So in 24 hours I went from dreaming of turning professional but never seriously considering it, to having two offers on the table.

The difference between the two offers was pretty evident. There were two GAN team cars at the world titles, Chris had his own mechanic and masseur, and I could see they were serious about their track program as well. During my meeting with the Polti guy he said he could also introduce me to his beautiful niece. It was a no-brainer to sign with GAN.

It was all confirmed during the 1994 Commonwealth Games in Canada. The team sent a heap of faxes through to the athletes' village and I signed my first deal for about AUD$50,000 a year. Coming from $20 a week with Charlie, I thought I was the king of the castle.

In January 1995 I left for Europe and my life changed forever. I said goodbye to Mum and Dad and flew to Germany to pick up a team car; all I had was a yellow sticky note with an address. I figured it was in Paris, and because there was no GPS in those days, I got completely lost. I stopped at a service station but by 10 pm I gave up and knocked on the door of a hotel. I couldn't speak a word of French so pointed to the address. Luckily for me, the guy jumped in his car and I followed him to where I was supposed to be going.

I got to my hotel at 11.30 pm, it was dark and I had to wake up the owners who were meant to be looking after me. The hotel was about 20 km outside of Paris with literally one bedroom, a tiny TV which I couldn't watch because it was in French, and a toilet.

I remember some nights just staring at the ceiling because back then we didn't have the internet, we didn't have laptops or smart phones for any outside information. Australia could have sunk and I wouldn't have known about it until someone wrote me a letter because even ringing home wasn't an option because it was so expensive. I was lucky to speak to Mum and Dad once a fortnight.

It really was the toughest two years of my life. I didn't have a clue about the language, the weather was diabolical, the training was a nightmare and I was lonely. The only thing that was pushing me was my determination to become a professional rider. In those early years I'd rock up to a race, get my arse kicked, then be in the car heading back to my accommodation. It was so different to what I'd experienced in the national track program, which was more like a football team where you were surrounded by people, you knew what time you were stretching, eating and training.

Now I was making up my own training programs, there was no coach and my training was basically damage control. I was getting my head kicked in on the bike, my confidence decreased and I'd succumb to eating and putting on weight. The only good part of my day was the dessert my hosts at home would serve me; the lady was an incredible cook. But there was nothing else to do. Eat, sleep and train. I only had one teammate who lived close by and he took me for a ride when I first arrived, but because I didn't speak French we couldn't converse; he must have thought I was pretty boring. Most of the time, I trained on my own. Riding was my freedom and even if it was crappy weather I'd still train for hours and tell myself it was the apprenticeship that I had to do if I wanted to be a big rider.

I felt homesick at times and had to fight a mental battle because I couldn't allow myself to think about going back to Australia. At the end of a race all my French teammates would pack up and go home to their families. The only English-speaking teammate was Chris Boardman who would jump on a plane and fly back to Manchester; I remember thinking, 'How lucky is that guy.' In my spare time I'd go to the service course which was a little old house. I'd sit there and watch the mechanic build bikes but there was no discussion because he spoke French and I didn't.

The highlight of my week was Friday night when I'd drive into the Champs Elysées, watch a movie in English and get McDonald's on my own. That was my night out. Slowly I started learning French, but only by picking up a few words at a time. Eventually I picked up enough to converse. When you're surrounded by a language, you have no choice. There was a game similar to *Sale of the Century* on TV called *Questions pour un Champion*, and I'd read every question and would learn about pronunciation.

I was on the road program but the agreement was to spend the first five months on the road, then go to the track with Charlie and the boys. I had all the pro kit and laid it on the bed. I'm sure I slept in the GAN jersey when I got it and thought it was awesome. But after the first training camp in super-cold conditions I got a knee injury trying to push it. This put me out for three months, which only made my first year in France even harder. I wanted to prove to the team that I was going well when suddenly I had to sit in the cold, in a shitty hotel, with a knee injury.

But I stuck it out over there. I was committed, I wasn't going to pack up and go home. I still managed to win two races—stages of smaller tours—which was pretty good for a neo-pro. The first one was in the Tour de L'Oise. We had a big team meeting the night before and my French sports director, Roger Legeay, would translate to English. We were to work for our sprinter, Christophe Capelle, and I had to lead him out.

The next day, as planned, it came down to the sprint. I hit out at 500 metres to go and as the finish line got closer, no one was coming past. 'Oh shit,' I thought because I knew Christophe was behind me but couldn't come past, so I hit the brakes, he won and I was second. That night my masseur, who spoke English, said to me, 'Don't you ever do that again. If you can win a race, you win, it's not your fault if he can't come past you.' But I was just following team orders and that night at dinner, Christophe was good enough to say thanks very much. The next morning in our meeting he said, 'Why don't we sprint for you?' And guess what? I ended up winning. That was such a monumental moment. It was not a big race by any means, just a French cup, but to have experienced a win, I knew things were going to be okay and I fed off that.

My first season as a professional cyclist in 1995 included my first Paris–Roubaix which lit a flame inside me that would burn for the best part of the next twenty years. It wasn't just my first Paris–Roubaix, it was my first Classic, but I'd been around the team long enough to understand that Paris–Roubaix was massive. We had a Frenchman in our team, Gilbert Duclos-Lassalle, who I used to call 'papa' because he was roughly double my age. He had won back-to-back Paris–Roubaix titles in 1992 and 1993 so I could see how seriously our team treated the race.

At the time of being selected I still hadn't seen any of the course and the famous Arenberg forest, but on our first reconnaissance mission I was shocked at how ridiculously hard it was riding the cobbles. If you've never ridden over cobblestones at top speed, when you're absolutely at your limit and in the freezing rain, it's very hard to describe what happens to your body. The bone-jarring sensation starts in your wrists and feet, then winds its way up your arms and legs and suddenly your shoulders are aching, your teeth are gnashing together, your eyes are watering and your head is bouncing around all over the place. But through the pain all you're thinking is, 'Keep going, keep pedalling, watch out for that drop, hold the wheel in front of you.' You're scanning the roads ahead of you like some crazed person in a computer game; one false manoeuvre, left or right, and bang, puncture means race over. Somehow you become oblivious to what your body is going through.

The night before my first Paris–Roubaix, we had a team meeting in our little hotel. I was shitting myself because I was told my job was to be in the first breakaway of the day. I thought, 'Holy crap, I've got to be in that first break, no pressure or anything.'

Riding to the start in the morning, it was cold and still foggy and I was nervous. But it was a good thing that I was on edge because I made sure I was with every single move that went in the first 30 km. I must have used up so much energy but I had to be in that first break, which finally got away after about half an hour when ten riders went clear of the peloton. The adrenaline rush was amazing and we rode in front for about 120 km before being caught on the fourth cobbled section. The first thing that warned me we were about to be caught was the noise—not the team cars or commissaires, but the bunch bearing down on us. It was like a hundred horses pounding the pavement, and before we knew it the peloton flew straight past, leaving us to fight our way through the dust storm. The race wasn't even halfway through and I was done. I'd gone from the front of the race to the back of the race in thirty seconds and there was no way out. Eventually I managed to get to the next feed zone at 140 km and just clicked out of my pedals, got off my bike and into the team car and said, 'What the hell am I doing in this sport? That was ridiculous.'

It might sound dramatic but I was seriously questioning whether I was kidding myself even being there. I thought, this game is obviously not for me; I'm good at the track and I can hold my own on the road, but there's no way I could go that fast over the cobbles. Even though I'd won some small races, the difference in the one-day Classics was monumental; it was pretty hardcore. Despite feeling like I'd failed that day, as far as the team was concerned, I'd done my job and when we sat around the bar that night, Duclos-Lassalle, who finished nineteenth, gave me a big hug and thanked me. In my eyes I hadn't gone far enough into the race but he said, 'Job was perfect, thanks.'

I eventually finished my second attempt at Paris–Roubaix in 1996 which helped me overcome some of the mental scars from the year before. Despite the pain and suffering, something about the race intrigued me. I don't know whether it was the history of Paris–Roubaix or the brutal pave which meant all-out war on a bike, but riding into the velodrome in Roubaix for the first time in 1996 was spine-tingling. After most races I would either ring home or send a fax so Mum and Dad could keep tabs on how I was going. The fax I sent that day reads:

> *I've pretty much recovered from the Hell of the North, what a day, what a race, words do little to describe the punishment I gave my body ... I was really counting the final kms down, absolutely knackered. But when I passed under the flame rouge for 1 km to go and entered the velodrome with 1000s of screaming spectators the feeling and emotions were incredible. It had*

always been a dream of mine to ride into that velodrome and when it happened I crossed the line and it was the biggest feeling of achievement I've yet felt.

I am quite content with my first proper effort at the Paris–Roubaix. In five years' time, who knows hey! No Aussie has ever won that race, you never know!

After my first little stint with the road team in 1995, I went back to the track. Because I'd been riding the road I could push a much bigger gear and we won the team pursuit world championship for the second time. I also managed to get bronze in the individual pursuit behind Chris Boardman and Graham O' Bree, so it was a perfect way to finish the year.

At the time, I still didn't know what kind of rider I was developing into and I don't think the team had any idea of what I was capable of either. I knew I wasn't a mountain climber but I was third in the world in the individual pursuit and we were team pursuit world champions so I guess they thought I might have been the next Chris Boardman, the next big time-trialler, but I could sprint and they just let me roll with it. They'd throw me in a race and see what happened.

That was the cool part of being with my director Roger Legeay; he was like my second dad. He was the key to my transition from track to road and vice versa. He didn't put any stress on me and took me under his wing. Whether it was a little experiment or whether he saw a bit of talent in me, he was really good.

Frenchman Legeay, a former professional cyclist and long-time team manager, had been monitoring Stuart's progress while he was in the Australian track program. He had spoken to Charlie Walsh and was in no doubt that Stuart would be able to transfer his 'very big talent' from the track to the road. But he knew it would not be easy. Legeay said European cyclists had a distinct advantage of turning professional in their own backyard while young Australians had to venture to the other side of the world.

'When he was nineteen years old and came with us, he was a boy, he was beginning in the professionals and it was very hard,' Legeay says. 'His family, they gave him to me and Stuart arrived in France with a bag and from the beginning we had a very good feeling with him and later with his family.

'I knew he had a big talent and if a rider like Stuart did everything well, I was sure he would have a very nice career.'

Almost twenty years later, they still keep in touch. 'Not many riders are my friends because they change teams and the like,' Legeay says. 'But with Stuart, every two or three months we text each other. He's a friend now, as is his family, there's a great history.'

By 1996, my standing at GAN began to change. When I got back to France we had our team photo and normally it's the big team captains in the middle of the poster but suddenly there I was standing in the middle with Chris Boardman in our world champion rainbow jerseys. It was a massive moment for me. I went back to live in the same hotel and 1996 was pretty much identical to my first season in terms of half on the road and half on the track.

But the focus was all on the Atlanta Olympics where it was decided I would do the points race and teams pursuit. We went there as defending world champions but in the end we didn't go fast enough as France took the gold medal from Russia. I was pretty devastated because I thought that would be my last Olympics—on the track at least—because road professionals were only allowed to race in the Olympics from 1996 and I hadn't even thought of making that team. I was hoping to do a bit better in the points race but I ended up winning two bronze medals. For the second straight Olympics, I was left with a bitter taste in my mouth. I still hadn't got the gold that I so desperately wanted. In Barcelona we'd come so close, but in Atlanta we were beaten fair and square. All that training, all that pain—and I still hadn't succeeded.

CHAPTER 3

A TERRIBLE DECISION

There wasn't a hint of sadness as I left the track for what I thought would be the final time in 1997 and became a full-time road cyclist. In fact, it was surprisingly easy to say goodbye to velodromes and Charlie's training programs, even though they had been such a big part of my life and was the reason I found myself on a professional road team in the first place. But it was time. After the Atlanta Olympics I'd had enough. It was as though I'd resigned myself to the fact that I'd done everything I could to get that gold medal but it wasn't enough. And as much as it hurt to miss out, I didn't want to commit to another four-year cycle with the track program.

So it was back to Europe to go full gas on the road, not really knowing what lay ahead of me. After my first two years in Paris I decided to say goodbye to the city's crap weather and lonely existence and moved to a little place on the north-east coast of Spain called L'Estartit. The accommodation was cheap because no one was around and it was fantastic for training because there were no distractions and the weather was 15–20 degrees warmer.

Now in my third season with the team, my wage started to improve. My new deal was almost double what my first two-year contract was worth and it was justified by my early-season form because I could focus 100 per cent on the road.

It started with the spring Classics. In my third attempt at Paris–Roubaix in 1997, I managed to finish seventeenth while two of my teammates, Henk Vogels and Frederic Moncassin, were in the top ten. It was on the cobbles that I noticed my track background was a massive advantage because I could spin my legs and maintain a high cadence. On the cobbles during races like Paris–Roubaix and Tour of Flanders it's all about keeping a fluid pedal stroke and trying to float across the uneven surface because if you're pushing a high gear, you lose momentum and you stop.

Stuart's smooth pedalling became one of his trademarks in the international peloton. German Jens Voigt, who rode alongside the Australian at GAN, CSC and Leopard-Trek, says it was one of the first things he noticed when he met him in 1998. Voigt's earliest memory of Stuart is of a 'little track kid, not chunky, but there was just more of him then'—and he was complete with blonde spiky hair and an earring.

'The first thing that impressed me was his smooth pedal-stroke, he was not even moving an ear,' Voigt says. 'Some people just have it. Like Dave Millar as well, he looks really good on a bike, even when he gets dropped he still looks good. I look shit when I get dropped. I look okay when I win.'

The other aspect of Stuart's career that continued to amaze Voigt was his ability to descend at frighteningly high speed. 'I'm still trying to work out if he is a gifted descender or just a daredevil,' Voigt remarks. 'I still haven't worked out if he really does know what he's doing or if he just goes, "I don't care, I just go." But he is a great bike-handler.'

My directors obviously liked what they saw in me throughout the rest of the 1997 spring because I was selected for the biggest race of all—I was to debut in the Tour de France. It was a pretty big deal for several reasons, not least because I was taking a Frenchman's spot, in a French team, for the Tour de France. And for it to happen at such a young age—twenty-three—it probably shocked a few of my teammates. But once again, Roger Legeay could see a bit of potential. I'd had a good season, done my job and he was giving me a chance.

From a pro bike-rider's point of view, making the Tour de France was bigger than being selected for the Olympic Games. The crowds are unbelievable and that's when I realised that this was on another level. I had never done a Grand Tour, maybe a Paris–Nice which is a one-week stage race, but my preparation certainly wasn't what it's like for young guys nowadays who are eased into the Giro d'Italia by racing for two weeks then pulling out. Back then, if you got a spot in the Tour de France, you had to get your arse to Paris.

For the first week of the race, it was like being in a dream. Chris Boardman won the prologue in Rouen then another teammate Cedric Vasseur took the yellow jersey on Stage 5 and kept it for six days. The day he took the jersey, Cedric was on his own and I jumped into a break behind him. Because I didn't have to work, I pumped them in the sprint and we took first and second—a momentous occasion for our team.

But it wasn't long until the race went into the mountains and I was hung out to dry. The speed of some of the guys in the peloton was phenomenal and I was dropped. Having the yellow jersey in the team didn't help my cause as I'd already done a lot of work on the front and was learning to maintain tempo for the breakaway, so when we got to the mountains I was nailed. And if I was exhausted when we hit the mountains, I was completely wasted by the time we got to Paris. I clearly remember every day in the mountains just saying to myself, 'I've got to get there, there's no way I'm pulling out.'

One of the biggest lessons I learnt in my first Tour de France was the value of your teammates. It was a big mountain day and after 5 km I was dropped with three sprinters. Then sure enough, about 10 km up the road, the sprinters I was with all stopped, clicked out and got in their team cars, leaving me on my own. I looked around in disbelief and thought, 'I can't do that,' so I just kept pedalling on my own, knowing the peloton and my chances of making it to Paris were getting further away. I kept going for another 10 km when suddenly I noticed a rider way off in the distance. At first I thought it was another victim of the pace at the front of the race but then I recognised his jersey. It was my team, and the closer he got I realised it was one of the older guys, Eros Poli. When I reached him I asked, 'What are you doing?' and he said, 'Just sit behind and don't panic.' He then began towing me for 180 km through the mountains. At one point I felt bad and went to go around him to help and he barked, 'Get back!' so I just sat on his wheel, kept a nice tempo and finally we caught the grupetto—the last bunch—on the last climb and scraped through the time cut by the skin of our teeth. It was the epitome of teamwork. At the time I thought, 'My God, we both could have been out of the race that night,' but he was so cool, calm and confident. I learnt a lot from Eros that day and it stuck in my head because I did it for many of my own teammates over the years. Cycling is all about the team—individuals don't last very long and that stage was one of the most punishing days of my life, but also one of the most significant.

Despite that, I still didn't know how I was going to make

it to Paris and the longer the race went, the harder it got. I would wake up in the morning and it hurt to get out of bed, it hurt to take those steps to go to breakfast and I would think, how the hell am I going to ride a 200 km stage? It doesn't matter how good a mountain climber you are, the speed of some of the guys was unbelievable. Maybe I was naïve, but I kept telling myself that the problem was I trained too much on the flat, I did too much sprint training and not enough in the mountains; I figured these guys were superheroes. But at the same time I was seeing guys doing this day in, day out and of course I questioned whether it was physically possible. But a part of me didn't want to believe they were cheating.

As far as I was concerned, doping was a taboo subject. No one openly talked about it and barely anyone spoke English, so even if it was discussed, I wouldn't have understood much. But even so, after a couple of years in the peloton I was aware that not everything was what it seemed and performance-enhancing drugs were out there. You're doing so many races throughout the year; eventually you find out what is going on. I began to notice that riders who had no real physical advantage or natural ability were suddenly becoming winners and doing phenomenal rides. There's an old saying, 'You can't turn a donkey into a racehorse' but I was seeing guys batting way above their average, doing ridiculous rides and I'd think, 'Where the hell did that come from?' But from what I now gather, the performance-enhancing drug Erythropoietin, or EPO, probably had something to do with it.

I finally made it to Paris and I was rapt; I certainly didn't think, 'I've got to get some assistance here.' I was just thrilled to finish my first Tour de France, having achieved something great after putting myself through hell; it was very satisfying. This time I wasn't coming in to the Champs Elysées to get McDonald's and go to the movies; I was finishing the Tour de France—albeit in 109th place and 3 hours 35 minutes and 56 seconds behind German winner, Jan Ullrich. It's a magical feeling to hear the crowd roar as you come around the corner onto the Champs Elysées; three weeks of pain and suffering goes out the window and is erased from your memory like wiping clean a hard drive.

The first thing the boys did when we got there was put beer in my water bottles. Each team does a lap of honour after a glass of champagne but the boys knew I liked beer so that's what went into my bidons. It's a tradition for every team to have a pretty large night celebrating when they get to Paris. Even though I've obviously never been in a war, the Tour de France is sport's version of a battle, and you sit there all night telling war stories. It's this tradition that has always stopped me from pulling out of the Tour because I knew that if I pulled out and abandoned the race, I'd be in the hotel sitting around the table and feeling like shit. It must be one of the most depressing moments of any cyclist's life because there's no hanging around to watch the race. You're flying home the next day. The closest I ever came to pulling the pin in my seventeen Tours de France—race-ending injuries aside—was in 2012 when I had a mechanical problem early, was dropped and had no way of making it back to the peloton on my own. I swear to God if my wife and kids weren't waiting for me in Paris, I would have pulled out but I knew I couldn't let them down so just kept pedalling.

If 1997 was a steep learning curve then 1998 was a turning point in my career. But it also involved a decision that I will regret for the rest of my life. I had ridden my first Tour de France and, as they say, 'With every grand tour you ride, the stronger you get.' I was coming off a good pre-season in Australia so I was ready for a big year on the road. The hard work paid off when I won my first ever stage race, the Tour of Britain, in May. Known as the Prudential Tour, it was considered a lead-up to the Tour de France. I won Stage 2 and Stage 7 and had three other podium finishes to win the race by 46 seconds, defeating Chris Boardman.

I was on a roll, which led to my selection in the Tour de France. But I was also scared because part of me didn't want to struggle like I had the year before. It's unnerving going into the Tour when you absolutely know that you're going to suffer for three weeks—just to make it to the finish.

Just before the Tour, most European riders race their national championships but, being Australian, I had about twelve days at my new home in Toulouse. That's when I agonised over the decision to experiment with EPO. I still can't recall exactly why I decided to go down this avenue— maybe I was intrigued by what all the fuss was about—but even before I got in my car to go and get it, I remember thinking, 'This goes against every moral grain in my body.' I had ridden the Olympics, I'd come up through the AIS and injecting even vitamins was against an Australian's nature. But in Europe, recovery with vitamin injections was common and legal, and I had previously been injected with Vitamin C to stay in a healthy state. But I don't know what pushed me to go further.

I remember sitting at home having a really big moral battle with myself; it was in steps. The first was to say, 'Okay, I'll try and find it.'

I never discussed using EPO with anyone, but when you're on the road with two hundred guys for two hundred days a year, you hear things, and at that time, there was a fair bit of talk about EPO being used in the peloton. No one ever approached me to talk about it or offer it to me and, similarly, I didn't approach anyone. That would have just opened up a whole new ball game because once you talk to someone about it, who do you trust?

I didn't research it, I didn't read up on it, I just joined the dots from what I could gather in the peloton that you only had to go to Spain to get it, and so I did. I didn't know much about it and, of course, I was shit scared about the health side-effects or going over the limit. But I figured if you took a lot, you'd be putting yourself at risk which is why I took the absolute minimum dose.

I didn't tell anyone where I was going or what I was doing; I felt terrible. When I got to the pharmacy in Spain, I sat in my car outside for God knows how long. It took me quite a few attempts to go in because I was so nervous and I knew that what I was doing was wrong. But still, I went in and decided to buy a small amount to take home. EPO is used to create red blood cells, which carry more oxygen, and it's generally used by people battling a big illness. But the pharmacist didn't ask what I needed it for or why I was buying it. So I grabbed a box, I can't remember what it cost, and some small syringes, and headed home.

While I had a few friends and teammates living with me in Toulouse, I only had one housemate but he wasn't there at the time because he was out of the country. So I was living on my own when I went down this path and, again, it was a lonely feeling at times. No one knew what I was doing.

Even though I had the EPO in my hands, my mental battle continued. It was a really shit moment. I sat there thinking of everything I'd done, my upbringing, the people who'd guided me ... but they weren't there; there was no one to bounce this off and I knew it was going to be a turning point. I was about to experiment with doping and the person I was about to cheat the most was myself. There was no one I could hurt any more than myself. Even thinking about it now, I still don't understand why I went down this avenue; it's an inexplicable decision.

I was about to re-negotiate my contract later that year and I loved racing as a professional but it was hardcore. It was definitely different from the dream I'd pictured when I got on a plane to fly to Europe. I thought there'd be a lot more people around to support me, not just because at times I was sad and lonely, but to physically train with. Furthermore, I didn't have a coach; I was left to my own devices. I was either at home, doing my race, or going home. Whatever led me to this moment—I don't know if desperation is the right word—but I didn't want to experience that degree of suffering in the Tour again. I wanted to be at the front, I wanted to win.

I was terrified about the possible side-effects on my health, I was freaking out and it went against all my morals; but still, I did it. Afterwards I remember feeling pretty flat. I was angry with myself but I didn't just do it once; I did it over a ten- to twelve-day period leading into the start of the Tour de France. I used it every second day because I was too afraid to do it every day. I'm sure if I didn't feel any improvement in my performance at the time, there would have been a placebo effect.

I don't want to be a rider who says, 'If you didn't get on board with doping you'd get dropped,' because that's an easy excuse. Ultimately, you've got to be held responsible for what you put in your body and everyone has the right to say no. But I wasn't strong enough and I gave in.

When I left home for the Tour de France, I put the EPO in my bag. It was pretty easy to hide one small vial but I was still scared. Buying it was challenging enough but travelling with it to Dublin for the start of the Tour was nerve-racking. It was like carrying a time-bomb; in my world what I'd done was as bad as it could get.

CHAPTER 4

BENEATH MY YELLOW JERSEY

If I was scared just going to the 1998 Tour de France, I was terrified when word trickled through that police had stopped a rival team car at the Belgian border and found it loaded with doping products. I was freaking out inside but at the same time trying to stay focused on my own race. I was thinking, 'Is this really happening? They're going through cars?' I definitely considered getting rid of the EPO in my bag, but what do you do? I was hiding it from my roommate and, to be honest, I didn't want to touch the stuff. I didn't want to risk getting it out, so I just left it there and the race started.

The 5.7 km prologue in Dublin was won by my teammate Chris Boardman, an amazing start for our team and the sponsors. But on Stage 2, while wearing the yellow jersey,

Chris crashed out and was stretchered off in a neck brace. It was devastating for him and it left our team in tatters. We were promptly given orders to go on the attack.

The next day I found myself in a winning breakaway and managed a top-five finish to the 167 km stage from Roscoff to Lorient, now back in France. I followed attack after attack, which used up plenty of energy, and in the end I didn't have the legs to contest the final sprint. I was now third on general classification and just three seconds behind leader Bo Hamburger, which was exciting but also devastating to be so close but so far. Did taking EPO before the Tour assist me that day? Probably yes, but to what extent, I can't say. It wasn't as if all of a sudden I just took off and left everyone behind in my wake. Although I had it with me at the race not even being three seconds off the yellow jersey tempted me to use it again because I was so scared of being caught, which in those days included going beyond the legal 50 per cent hematocrit limit. (Hematocrit is a measure of red blood cells in your system.) I didn't have a doctor, and I figured that if you took it during the race, you'd be busted and gee, that would ruin your life, wouldn't it?

Stage 4 was a 252 km, mostly flat, trek from Plouay to Cholet, the longest stage of that year's Tour. As we approached one of the bonus sprints with Mario Cipollini, Erik Zabel and other legends in the bunch, all I needed was a couple of seconds over George Hincapie on the road to take the yellow jersey. I knew that I was quicker than George so I mustered up enough courage to go over to

Cipollini—who I'd never spoken to in my life because he was this big, scary Italian God—and said, 'Mario, is it okay if you don't sprint, just let me win?' He looked at me and said, 'We'll see.' Right, that was one taken care of, now I had to find Zabel. So I rode up to him and said, 'Erik, is it okay if you let me win the sprint? It's for the yellow jersey, man.' His reply was, 'Okay, but as long as I get second,' because he was still thinking about the green jersey and had a very mathematical process about how he went for it.

These guys were superstars of the sport and would have had no idea who I was, but I went around to every sprinter who was going for the green jersey and asked them not to sprint for the next time bonus so I could be in yellow. They were obviously feeling generous because as the race was all together, I ended up winning the sprint. Now all I had to do was get to the finish and I had the yellow jersey in the Tour de France. I collected two of the three six-second time bonuses that day and was the virtual race leader.

We were at the front of the group trying to stay out of trouble. Everything was looking pretty good and guys were coming up to say congratulations when Australian Neil Stephens rode up next to me and said, 'Just be really careful in the final, it gets dodgy.' For the rest of the stage I was crapping myself and, sure enough, with a kilometre and a half to go, disaster struck.

The rule used to be that if you crashed inside the last 1 km you got the same time as the winner. Now it's 3 km. But this day we came around a bend with 1.5 km to go and there was a massive crash. Bang, and suddenly I'm in the barriers. I have no idea what happened but the next thing I knew I was on the ground and freaking out. I grabbed my bike, jumped on and Stevo appeared out of nowhere and yelled, 'Jump on Stuey!' and sprinted me towards the peloton. The bunch was blown to pieces but he towed me back to the front group and I got the yellow jersey pretty much thanks to Stevo that day. Not a very glamorous way to claim the biggest prize in world cycling—halfway through the race and after a crash in the final few kilometres—but it was a total adrenaline rush. In the space of a minute, my thinking went from, 'Far out, I've got the jersey!' to 'I can't lose it like this,' and panicking. We were going so fast at the end that it was pure relief when we caught them before the finish.

I became the second Australian to wear the yellow jersey at the Tour de France and first since Phil Anderson in 1982. I was now the overall leader by eleven seconds, which meant absolute chaos after the stage. A good chaos, but it was very surreal getting chaperoned back to the podium, people everywhere and cameras in your face. One of my quotes to reporters after the race was 'Who would have thought a freckly bastard like me would be wearing this beautiful jersey?' I felt like I was inside a big washing machine of emotion, but no one knew that I was hiding a dark secret. Yes, I'd made a decision that went against my moral judgement, but I was so caught up in the circus of the Tour de France that everything seemed very surreal. I felt like I was in Disneyland but the dream didn't last long.

As far as I can remember, back then it was the race leader,

stage winner and a few random riders who were drug-tested. Walking into doping control and peeing into the cup straight after that stage was one of the scariest moments of my life. My hands were shaking as I didn't know whether the EPO was still in my system. Things got even worse when I arrived back at the hotel and heard what had happened with the Festina team: guys were getting arrested and taken away by the police. Watching events unfold on French TV was the final straw. To say I was scared is an understatement; I was petrified. I was wearing the yellow jersey in the Tour de France, I had a vial of EPO in my bag and guys were getting arrested. What more of a slap across the face did I need? The price of being caught with this stuff was being taken away in handcuffs.

I know there are people who question whether I doped later in my career, but having witnessed the events of that Tour, I knew that to do it again I would have to be insane.

When my roommate went for a massage that night I got the EPO out of my bag, smashed it and flushed it down the toilet. Even though the damage was done, it was as if I was flushing away some of my sins. I swore to myself that I would never take EPO again.

With the yellow jersey hanging over a chair in my room, I put my inner turmoil aside and called my parents who were home in Adelaide where it was the early hours of the morning. In those days they didn't broadcast the Tour de France on TV.

Stuart's father Brian has kept a diary almost every day of his adult life. Documenting the night of 15 July 1998, when Stuart took the yellow jersey is the following entry:

Well, Stu rang us at 0230hrs to tell us it's really true, he is the official leader of the Tour de France. He was so happy and reckoned he was going to sleep in the yellow jersey. It was so fantastic to hear him so happy and such a turnaround from his earlier phone call. Oh my God, the yellow jersey.

My family was obviously pretty excited about the news. Anyone else who called home that day was greeted with a new answering machine message saying: 'Hello, you have reached the home of the yellow jersey'—which was Lesley's idea.

Back at the Tour, I went to sleep that night feeling confused, questioning myself, 'Did I need to do that? Surely I could have achieved that without EPO, I'm sure I could have.' But it was too late. The circus continued the next morning when I walked outside the hotel to find thousands of people saying, 'The maillot jaune, the maillot jaune!' They didn't even know who I was; all they wanted was to touch and smell the yellow jersey; that is the power of the biggest prize in cycling.

Now that we had the yellow jersey back, the team wanted

to keep it for as long as possible and I certainly didn't want to give it away. I managed to wear it for three days and it was so stressful. You have to go back to the podium after each stage when all your teammates are back on the bus eating and having a shower. Then they're relaxing while you're at doping control, doing interviews with local media, international media, your country's media—it seems like an eternity.

The first day was Stage 5, a hectic 228.5 km from Cholet to Châteauroux, and I went down in a crash just before the first intermediate sprint at the 80 km mark. I had some pretty bad skin grazing on my arms and hip and battled on to finish fifteenth behind stage winner Mario Cipollini, but George Hincapie had cut my lead from eleven to seven seconds.

Stage 6 was 204 km from La Châtre to Brive-la-Gaillard which was easier to negotiate and I still led overnight, but not without an early fright after missing the start because I was so caught up in the emotion of wearing the yellow jersey that I got carried away signing autographs before the stage. Eventually I had to hand the yellow jersey to Jan Ullrich on the Stage 7 individual time-trial. I rode one of the best time-trials of my life in super-hot weather and on tiny, hilly farm roads but I did the jersey relatively proud to finish fifteenth.

By then, I thought the highs of my Tour de France were over but another day of reckoning came on Stage 14 when I found myself in another breakaway on a hilly 186.5 km stage from Valréas to Grenoble. I just held on over the last climb of the day and descended like mad, trying to drop a few of the guys coming into the finish. Then suddenly, a few of them attacked with 2 to 3 km to go and a couple of other guys just sat up as if to say they were done and couldn't be bothered chasing. I said, 'What are you guys doing, we've been out here for 180 km and now you're going to stop?' That was the win right there as two guys kept riding away from us in the breakaway. So I got everyone organised and said, 'Come on, come on,' trying to get them to believe that there was still an opportunity because no one wants to come third. This was the chance for a stage victory at the Tour de France—something I had never experienced despite being the race leader for three days the week before.

The guys with me started to realise that we might actually catch them and with under 1 km to go we did. The finish line got closer and by now there was no worrying about anyone else, this stage was mine. I timed my sprint, gave it absolutely everything and no one could go past me. It was an unbelievable feeling, I had just won a stage of the Tour de France! I can't say whether the EPO still had an effect, but I cleared the doping controls so who knows. More podiums, more flowers, more interviews, more cameras and more madness. I was back in the washing machine of emotion, still not really knowing what to think.

Celebrations were fairly restrained that night, a glass of champagne was all we were allowed and, surprisingly, that was all I wanted because the next day we were back in the mountains swinging for our lives again. It was a punch in the head that brought a reality-check—one day you're the king of the castle, the next day you're just another rider getting dropped. That's the emotion of the Tour and for me, riding it for just the second time having worn the yellow jersey and won a stage in the first two weeks, it was even more pronounced.

While the race continued, so did police investigations into doping in the peloton; in fact, the drama seemed to engulf the Tour. By now the Festina team had been kicked off the race and three days after my stage win in Grenoble, things came to a head.

On 29 July we were on the road for Stage 17, on the way from Albertville to Aix-les-Bains, when all of a sudden the peloton slowed down and guys hopped off their bikes and sat on the road. It was a sit-down protest against the treatment of the riders at Dutch team TVM who were being investigated. I had no idea what was going on. Then the next minute we were back on our bikes riding up the mountain again when word came through the peloton that they'd neutralised the stage.

It was a very weird time for cycling. Riders were protesting, spectators were booing us and teams were talking of abandoning the Tour. It was a perfect illustration of cycling's bubble: some of the protesting riders were doping but they dealt with the stress by going on the offensive. As for me: I knew what I'd done, but I just wanted to keep out of it. Looking back on it now, the whole situation was farcical.

With so many points in breakaways I ended up finishing second in the green jersey when we got to Paris four days later. My Tour de France was over and as successful as it was, I was relieved it had finished. I had cheated, I had got away with it by the skin of my teeth and I wanted to erase it from my mind. I didn't ever want to tell anyone I'd done it, I definitely wasn't proud of it, it was the worst decision I'd made in my life and I didn't ever want to be in that situation again.

I realise that not everyone is going to believe me because in cycling so many people have lied for so long that people are sceptical. I'm never going to change their judgement. All I can say is that the battle I fought with myself was far bigger than any bike race could ever be.

Some riders who cheated their entire careers most likely needed to have some serious back-up because a lot of people are involved. I was very fortunate to have great directors and support from people who didn't advocate doping so I was never tempted to go down that path again. I certainly wasn't prepared to repeat the personal hell I'd experienced.

The 1998 Tour de France sky-rocketed me to the top but our sport went into the darkest moments of its history. I was more than happy to make it to Paris so I could start again and focus on something else.

At the Commonwealth Games in Kuala Lumpur, the Aussie team helped my good mate Jay Sweet win the road race. I was hoping to join him with a gold medal around my neck after the time-trial but it didn't go to plan. I went off in the first wave because it was super-hot, 90 per cent humidity, along with guys from countries I'd never even heard of wearing sneakers and on road bikes, but I was totally focused.

I was on the limit every pedal-stroke so it wasn't all that surprising when, coming downhill way too fast, I misjudged a corner, the front wheel went and I hit the deck, ripping my left side to pieces. I snapped my bike, blood was streaming out of me and I've still got the scars up my leg. I quickly got a road bike and finished the last 20 km in a world of pain, crossed the finish line and went straight to the medical centre. Through a blur of pain-killers I heard people saying, 'You've still got the fastest time.' Then the second wave went through and they said, 'Still got the fastest time.' I almost wanted someone to hurry up and smash it. The winner, Canadian Eric Wohlberg, ended up beating me by ten seconds but I was still pleased with my efforts when I headed home.

At that time, cycling in Australia wasn't as mainstream as it is now, and my achievements at the Tour de France provided a massive boost for the sport. I attracted a lot of media attention in Adelaide and there were accolades, congratulations and pats on the back. And yes, I happily took those pats on the back despite what I'd done. I still carried my dark secret; I buried it deep in my mind and hoped it would go away.

CHAPTER 5

SMASHED, BASHED AND CRASHED

When news broke that the inaugural Tour Down Under would be held in January 1999, I was straight on the phone to Roger Legeay trying to convince him to bring our team to Adelaide. Back then it wasn't a World Tour race but I'd known the race director, Mick Turtur, since I was a teenager and really wanted to be a part of it. But for a European team to come to Australia was basically unheard of at that time, and I think if you ask Roger now, it was probably more out of respect to me that he not only sent our team down under but he came as well.

It was the start of a new season but the events of the previous year weren't so easily forgotten. I'd played with fire, almost got my fingers burnt, and I was angry at myself for going down that path in the first place. I knew deep down that I could get results without resorting to doping so I was desperate to be fit for the Tour Down Under. It was a dream come true to have a race in my own backyard and I knew the roads around Adelaide like the back of my hand.

The Tour Down Under was a really good way for me to kick off the season, of equal importance to me psycho-logically as it was physically. December and January were the building blocks of my season. I would start training in November and, with my coach/trainer Leigh Bryan, I'd go to the AIS in Adelaide and use the gym facilities for the whole month and ride every second day. In the early years I'd link up with Luke Roberts, Jay Sweet and his brother Corey and we'd head out into the hills and rip four or five hours which had me in great shape for not only the national championships but for the Tour Down Under.

You go through a real high in the Tour Down Under, there's no external stress from the race organisation, you're eating at the same hotel every night, and it's the only race like it all year. My friends in Adelaide think every race on the calendar is like the Tour Down Under, and they say, 'Mate, you've got an awesome life.' But I tell them, 'This never happens again for the year.' You're constantly moving hotels, packing your suitcase, transferring between stages and not eating until 8.30 or 9 pm.

When the inaugural race rolled around, no one quite knew how it would be received in Adelaide. To my sur-prise, something like 50,000 people turned up to the first criterium. I rode around the corner, saw a sea of people and went, 'Holy shit!' At that point I'd only won one stage race in my career, the 1998 Tour of Britain, so week-long races weren't quite my thing and I thought I'd be happy just to win a stage.

I got through the criterium, which doubled as Stage 1, without any dramas and the next day sprinted to third place behind Erik Zabel in Stage 2 to Strathalbyn. Then it all happened on Stage 3 when I'd basically conceded that it wasn't going to be my day. I went away with the break on the road from Glenelg to Victor Harbor and by the time we got to Cement Hill with a group of ten, I thought it would be the race-winning move. But eventually a couple of teams worked on the front of the peloton to chase us down and just before the race was about to come back together, Phil Liggett, who was commentating on the road, came up to me in the car. He said, 'Oh well mate, what are you going to do now?' I just shrugged my shoulders and said, 'There's always tomorrow.'

As I was talking I realised that I'd slipped off the back of the breakaway so I forgot about Phil and quickly sprinted to get back on. When I got there I felt surprisingly good and decided to attack. We didn't have anything to lose because the bunch was bearing down on us, but it was one of those spontaneous decisions and it paid off. Because the peloton had worked so hard to catch us, they were all nailed and when they caught the break they didn't realise that I had taken off again. By this stage I was a minute up the road and riding my heart out to stay away. I ended up holding them off to win the stage which put me in the lead by eleven seconds which I extended to fifteen seconds when I won Stage 5 from Nuriootpa to Tanunda. I finished second on the final day through the Adelaide CBD to claim the inaugural Tour Down Under by 21 seconds.

I know it's not the Tour de France but for a kid from Adelaide to win the first big bike race around my home streets was an achievement I'll never forget. It was a magical moment and a dream start for the race to have a local boy win first up.

When July came around it was time to return to the Tour de France for a third time. After the 1998 affair, I figured the peloton would've had a big kick up the arse and everyone would be racing on the same level: clean. To me, it seemed inconceivable that guys would continue doping through 1999—how would they transport it, get through controls and more testing? I was sure the EPO era had gone. Evidently, that was far from the case.

I wore the green jersey in the Tour for three days and was sixteen seconds off the race lead when I sat second overall after Stage 4—but that was as close as I got to wearing yellow. I had a huge battle with Zabel in the points classification; on three separate sprint finishes I was one place behind him. I was also one place behind Mario Cipollini twice and was fourth on the Champs Elysées, which was won by Robbie McEwen, but I just didn't have the top-end speed to come around them.

For those who don't know how the green jersey works, it's the prize for leading the points classification at the Tour de

France. While the overall race leader wears yellow, the fast men compete for green—the ultimate prize for a sprinter. Points are awarded to the first riders across the line every day, and to those who are the first across the line in intermediate sprints out on the road. Zabel, who was so calculating about when and where he would accumulate points, went on to win his fourth straight green jersey while I was second, 48 points behind. The 1999 Tour also marked the first of Lance Armstrong's seven Tour de France victories while I was 94th, 2 hours and 30 minutes behind him.

Henk Vogels vividly remembers riding the 1999 Tour de France in support of Stuart and says that the events following it sparked his decision to leave GAN (which had changed its name to Crédit Agricole). He felt that Stuart did not do enough behind closed doors to keep him at the team.

'I wouldn't say we ended up on bad terms but I was a little disappointed with how I left the team in 1999,' Vogels says of his friendship with Stuart.

'Stuey was racing for the green jersey and I led him out every day, for every sprint stage and every intermediate sprint. Some of the other guys on the team wouldn't even get him a fucking water bottle.

'So I led him out for three weeks and at contract time at the end of the Tour, I asked Stuey to put in a good word for me with the team to renew my contract. Stuey had just signed a new deal with the team when Roger Legeay sat me down and said I'd got no results and I would be getting a one-year contract extension but it [money] would be cut in half. I literally told him to get fucked and I left.

'Looking back, I'm really stoked that I ended up moving to America and I signed for more than what I was on [at Crédit Agricole] anyway. But I was a bit pissed, more with Roger than with Stuey, because in the end he can't dictate what the team does. It just left a sour taste in my mouth after an awesome three years. It didn't end our friendship and the following year we rode the Sydney Olympics road race together so there are plenty of good memories.'

After the Tour, my teammate Henk Vogels decided to leave GAN. This was a really tough period because I was not only losing a teammate but also my best mate. Henk was one of the most loyal teammates I ever had, along with Matt White. Both blokes would sacrifice themselves 100 per cent for you. I think it's a part of the Australian mentality, but with Henk it went further than that. We rode the Classics together in the early years of my career and if anyone deserved to win a Classic, he did. After races like Paris–Roubaix we'd get the same plane home together, have a beer and talk about the race and I'd say, 'Henk, you could win this.' So it was really difficult when things didn't work out. I was getting a big offer from Roger Legeay and Henk probably doesn't know half the phone calls I had with Roger, telling him I was holding off on signing until Henk got his deal.

But it's tough, teams back you into a corner and, rightly or wrongly, I've always done my own contract negotiations. This time I had one of my best mates hanging on my word and when I eventually re-signed with the team it would have been nice to blame it on my manager, but I couldn't. I had a big offer on the table and that's when cycling becomes more than just a sport, it becomes a business.

Henk moved to America and I really missed him. We grew apart but he will always be one of those blokes who you might not see for six months, then when you catch up, it's like you saw each other yesterday.

Funnily enough, four years later I experienced exactly what Henk had gone through when I left Crédit Agricole; Roger and I didn't end on good terms. That's what happens when business gets in the way of friendship. It was the final week of the 2003 Tour de France, we were negotiating my contract and I could tell that Roger was hesitant. The Tour de France is where all the negotiating is done—every year I'd finalise my contract on the TGV on the way to Paris, and it was pretty consistent. I'd always roll over a two-year deal and the money would basically double every time because I was winning. But in 2003 the deal hadn't been done and I felt the vibe on our last night in Paris at the post-Tour party. We had a young Thor

Hushovd coming through and by now he was a better sprinter than I was, which he was proving day in, day out, so my role was slowly changing. I started aiming for the Classics and needed the whole team to support me.

I went home on the Monday after the Tour thinking, 'Something is not right here.' I had a gut feeling that I needed to move on. So I decided I would throw out a ridiculous figure—deep down hoping that Roger would say no—and then I could leave the team.

But the reason we finished on bad terms is that after nine years of my loyalty and Roger being like a second father figure to me, he just rang me and said, 'Look, we haven't got a place for you on the team.' I was standing in my home in Toulouse when he said that the budget was

spent. I was pretty pissed off that he didn't tell me face-to-face. I said to him, 'Well, if the budget is spent there was never any negotiating going to take place. You'd already made your decision so why didn't you man-up and tell me?' All I wanted was a hand-shake and for him to say, 'It's been a fantastic venture, look at what we've achieved but it's time to move on' and I would have felt exactly the same way. But instead he led me to believe there was always a position there when, in actual fact, he'd made up his mind.

I thought back to Henk and another teammate, Magnus Backstedt, who'd been through the same thing. Suddenly I was on the receiving end and it's not a nice feeling. I've seen it a lot in my career; many cycling managers are old bike-riders, they're not businessmen. They're not really

good at one-on-one communication when it comes to
ending contracts and saying, 'Au revoir.'

So I got off the phone to Roger, really annoyed, and
that's when it hit me: 'Holy shit, I've got to find another
team!' I remember Lance Armstrong coming up to me in
the Tour one year as we came into Paris, saying, 'Stuey, it's
about time you changed teams and came to a big team.'
I looked at him and said, 'What do you mean? I'm on a
big team.' He replied, 'No you're not, you're on a small
team.' Lance did ask me to come to US Postal a couple
of times, but I looked at his team and saw all eight guys
riding on the front every day in the mountains of the
Tour de France and thought there was absolutely no way
I could ever do that so there wouldn't even be a position
for me. So I'd just say, 'No worries Lance, thanks,' and
nothing ever came of it.

Eventually I ended up finding my way to another French
team, Cofidis, where I spent the 2004 and 2005 seasons
riding alongside Dave Millar and where I had some of
the best results of my career with another Tour de France
stage win, consecutive top-five finishes in Milan–San
Remo and, of course, the Athens Olympics.

But back to 1999: life was pretty good in Toulouse and
on 9 September I went out for tea with Henk, Dave and
our girlfriends to a Japanese restaurant in the city. We had
a few drinks and were walking down the main boulevard
in Toulouse at about 12.30 am. I was a couple of paces
ahead of the others and suddenly I noticed three guys
walking straight at me, not looking like they were going

to deviate. So I tried to walk between them, but one of the guys swiped at my neck and whipped off a gold necklace that my mum had given me. I instantly swung around, grabbed him around the throat and smashed him against a parked car, demanding that he give my chain back. I was punching above my weight because this guy was 20-odd kilograms bigger than me but I didn't care. Things were still fairly calm and I thought I had the situation under control but the girls started freaking out.

Just as I turned around to tell the girls to calm down, the guy I was holding had pulled the windscreen wiper off the parked car and cracked me over the head with the metal motorised section. Henk and Dave then came in with arms and legs going everywhere, not that I remember any of it, but I'm told there were a few misguided karate kicks and haymakers because Henk ended up getting himself dropped as well. All I remember is seeing a lot of blood coming from my head then waking up in hospital.

I managed to get a fractured skull and blood clot on the brain out of it, which was pretty nasty and ended my season. The most unbelievable thing about the incident was that it happened right in the middle of the boulevard in downtown Toulouse. There were people everywhere as it was a stock-standard time of the night in Europe to be coming home from a restaurant. Because it was in full view of plenty of people the cops were called and they managed to catch the guys. I had the opportunity to go to court and press charges, but I eventually decided to let it slide because I didn't need these guys knowing where I lived and I just wanted to get on with my cycling. I spent a week in hospital and recovered enough from my injuries to get back on the bike but I had ongoing troubles with the blood clot on my brain which was a few centimetres in size.

Later that year when I got back to Australia I flew to Noosa for a sponsor's ride. I was pinning on my number when my vision became really blurry and I passed out. I'd had a seizure and ended up in hospital. You only need one of them to scare the crap out of you, but it happened again ten years later at the 2009 Valencia MotoGP. I was good mates with Anthony Peden, who was a track sprinter for Australia before he moved to Europe and became Casey Stoner's personal trainer.

I'd been talking to Anthony about going to a MotoGP race for ages because I'm an adrenaline junkie—I've jumped out of a plane, been in a fighter jet, a V8 Super-car and bungee-jumped. But one of the things on my wish-list was to be on the back of a two-seater MotoGP bike. Anthony, who we call 'Weapon', messaged me the night before the Valencia round and said, 'Mate, have I got a surprise for you. Don't have a night out and don't eat too much for breakfast.' He'd organised for me to go on the back of a Ducati with Randy Mamola.

The following day, shaking like a leaf, I got kitted out in the leather gear and signed a waiver that if I died, it wasn't their fault. We cruised out of the pits and I thought, 'This isn't too bad.' But then he hit the throttle and I was hanging on for grim death, convinced I'd be sent sprawling across the track. Then we were up on the front wheel and I was riding Randy's back, being thrown around by G-forces you cannot imagine. I later found out we hit 280 km/h on the back straight. I was trying to turn my head to look at the crowd but it was a blur of colour and noise. We did the lap, had photos and I was still shaking from the adrenaline.

As I started walking back to the hospitality tent I got blotchy vision and it was getting worse. I sat down and a guy walked over to me and introduced himself but I couldn't see who it was. That's all I can remember. The next thing I knew, I woke up in hospital. When I came to they told me I'd had a seizure and had to stay in hospital for tests. Casey Stoner came in one night with his now wife Adrianna and brought me McDonald's—I so appreciated that he took time out to visit me, I'll never forget it. According to the doctors, the blood clot on my brain had left scar tissue and because the helmet was really right, combined with the G-forces and blood pressure, it triggered a seizure. It was all pretty freaky but I lived to tell the tale.

Once I'd recovered from my head injury in 1999, I geared the following season towards the 2000 Sydney Olympics. I wasn't in the best shape as I made a tentative return to racing but I had enough kilometres in the legs to ride the Tour de France in July, which would serve as the perfect preparation for both the points race and road race in Sydney soon after.

Things were going pretty well in the Tour until Stage

6—a 198 km flat stage from Vitre to Tours— when every-thing went horribly wrong. A spectator on the roadside banged a drum, making a booming sound which rippled through the peloton, eventually causing a crash. Sud-denly I went over the handlebars, landed on my shoulder and was on the ground in a world of pain. But as you do, I jumped up, grabbed my bike and the race doctor came over to have a look at me. I wasn't expecting to get the all-clear but he said, 'You're okay,' and off he went.

It's hard to explain the mental state you're in when you crash because of all the adrenaline, pain and emotions of the Tour de France coursing through your body. Under no circumstances do you want to pull out. Ever. The doctor was telling me my collarbone wasn't broken and even though I knew deep down that it was, I got back on my bike and rode 90 km to the finish in central France. For the first 10 to 15 km I tried to get out of the seat in an attempt to catch up to the bunch but I couldn't because my shoulder was absolutely killing. I couldn't put any pres-sure on my right arm so I draped it over the handlebars like I was in the time-trial position. A couple of guys who were in the same crash but from different teams waited for me and were pushing me up the climbs, which shows the camaraderie between cyclists when they're out on the roads together. By 20 km after the crash, the adrenaline had worn off and I was in absolute agony. I should have stopped, clicked out and left the race with a broken col-larbone but I didn't. I finished inside the time cut, which was an epic in itself, but the last 20 km of that day on 6

July 2000, I was in a world of pain that I didn't even know existed.

Cyclists seem to have an astonishingly high pain threshold and the Tour de France takes it to a new level. I've seen guys in neck braces, guys with half their skin missing and with cracked vertebrae—but they're still pedalling. That's what it means for a bike-rider, especially during the Tour de France. Unlike other sports, like soccer for instance, there's no showboating in cycling and there's no interchange bench to go and have a rest. You're either in or you're out, and every pedal-stroke is one closer to the finish: a motto I adopted throughout my career. Eventually you get from A to B and you pray to God that you're in the time cut.

When I finally made it to the finish that day I went straight from my bike to the ambulance where people were looking at me and wondering what the hell I'd just done. Scans in hospital showed that I'd broken my collarbone in three places, which would require surgery to insert a pin to hold it in place. There was no denying it any longer: my Tour was done. Even though the Sydney Olympics was only a month away, all I cared about was the Tour de France. I was devastated at having to abandon, especially because of a crash caused by someone hitting a drum. But more often than not, it's the stupid things that cause crashes. We're racing centimetres away from each other for thousands of kilometres but it's normally people jumping on the road or on the roadside drinking wine and getting pissed that cause the accidents.

Spectators put their chairs on the road and they don't realise that at 50 or 60 km/h, we take up every single centimetre of bitumen. It's bloody scary because you're only just missing people at really high speed and hitting the brakes quickly—the most common cause of crashes in the bunch.

When the disappointment of pulling out of the Tour de France for the first time finally abated, I worked out that I had six weeks to get ready for the Olympics. So a few days later I was on the home-trainer in the garage in Toulouse with a makeshift harness made out of old tyres wrapped around a beam to hold me upright. I had a couple of cushions on the handlebars to rest my right arm and as long as my legs could turn over, I told myself I was still in with a chance to make it to Sydney.

It took about twelve days on the home-trainer until I was ready to go back out on the road, then it took me another twenty minutes just to get out of the driveway. It's a mental thing because even though you know you're okay, you're worried that one bump, one sharp turn or unexpected stop will put pressure on the collarbone which was still healing.

Once I was out the driveway there was no looking back. I made it over the first bump safely and figured if I could do that, I could get over one hundred bumps so it was game on. It's amazing how quickly your body can mend and how psychological the whole recovery process can be. Even when I had my massive crash in the 2007 Tour de France, as I lay in intensive care with tubes poking out of me everywhere, I said to myself, 'Right, I'll be good for the Vuelta, I'll be good for the worlds.' I wanted to make myself believe that it was possible even though my team director probably thought I was crazy.

I've always believed that no matter how bad the situation or how much of a nightmare you're in, you've got to look for the positives and try to think that everything happens for a reason. That's been one of the biggest mottos of my entire life—that when you're down and out and you miss a race, it only makes you hungrier. So when you come back, you're better prepared for the next year because you start training harder, you don't take things for granted, you look after yourself and then the next thing you know, you've won an Olympics or a world cup or a stage of the Tour. So then you realise that missing a couple of months might've helped you towards this achievement.

As unlikely as it seemed when I sat on the trainer in my garage, held up by a few old bike tyres while nursing a broken collarbone, I made it to the Sydney Olympics for the 27 September road race—just over five weeks after my crash.

The Olympic road race was a tough 239 km and, admittedly, I didn't have a great day. Jan Ullrich won and I was 7:06 further back in 77th place. A week earlier I lined up in the points race on the track and managed to get 26 points but the winner, Juan Llaneras from Spain, took two laps and the gold medal with it while I finished tenth. I fully admit that I wasn't anywhere near my peak condition on the track, but Scott McGrory, who usually rides the points race, was rested up to stay fresh for the madison with Brett Aitken and they went on to win a gold medal. I remained in Sydney for the closing ceremony then flew back to Europe to suffer through until the end of the season. My third Olympics and still no gold medal but after what I'd been through in the previous twelve months—a blood clot on the brain, fractured skull and broken collarbone—I was just happy to still be riding my bike.

CHAPTER 6

PODIUM GIRL, WIFE OF MY DREAMS

How many men can say they met their wife while standing on the podium after a cycling race? Anne-Marie was a podium girl the day I won the most aggressive rider's jersey after Stage 1 of the 2000 Tour Down Under. A kiss from Anne-Marie was enough to motivate me to attack every stage for the rest of the week so I could get back on the podium. Unbeknown to us at the time, that brief meeting was the start of our lives together.

By the time I got back to the hotel that night my teammates had already eaten so I was at a table by myself when, coincidentally, the same two podium girls walked past. Naturally, I asked them to join me and I found out that

Anne-Marie was from Adelaide, doing a bit of model-ling, and knew absolutely nothing about cycling. I was the defending Tour Down Under champion but she had no idea who I was, which suited me fine.

I'd always gone out with European girls because they tend to understand cycling and the sacrifices riders have to make. I never thought I'd marry an Aussie girl because I assumed they'd never want to live on the other side of the world. But when I dated a few girls from Europe, their families got too involved and became almost like stalkers; it was all too weird for me.

So I eventually found the courage to ask Anne-Marie if she'd go out with me, and on the Tuesday night of the Tour Down Under, just as I was leaving the hotel, Roger Legeay caught me walking out way too dressed up for just a coffee with the boys. 'Where are you going?' he said. 'Oh, just for a coffee,' I replied. He looked at me sceptically and said, 'You're pretty well dressed to be going out for a coffee.' He knew exactly what was going on so I said, 'Look, I'll win for you tomorrow.' We shook on it and that was it.

Things between me and Anne-Marie went pretty well, and by the end of the week when it was time for me to head back to Europe I had some thinking to do. We chatted on the phone every day once I was in France, but soon enough we decided it would be a lot cheaper to fly Anne-Marie over. It was a massive show of faith from her family—allow-ing her to fly to the other side of the world to live with a guy they had only met once. I was on the road a lot with the team but we had our own community in Toulouse because

Stuart O'Grady, at age 14, about to start the time trial in the 1987 'two-day tour' at One Tree Hill just outside Adelaide.

Stuart, in his Port Adelaide Cycling Club colours and wearing the number one, prepares to start a race on his first proper bike, a red Elizabeth Star.

Stuart (centre) with brother Darren and their father Brian preparing to go on holiday with bikes loaded on the back of the family car.

With Australian teammates at the closing ceremony of the 1992 Barcelona Olympics: Damian McDonald, Stuart, Shaun O'Brien, Brett Aitken, Henk Vogels and Gary Niewand.

A disappointed Stuart, second from left, with his Australian teammates after losing the gold medal ride-off to Germany in the team pursuit at the 1992 Olympics.

Stuart shows off one of his bronze medals, from the points race, at the 1996 Atlanta Olympics.

Celebrating with Graeme Brown after their Olympic gold medal in the madison in 2004.

Stuart leads the breakaway during the 2012 London Olympic men's road race.

Stuart prepares for a track race with long-time cycling coach Charlie Walsh.

1993 team pursuit world champions: Brett Aitken, Tim O'Shannessy, Billy Joe Shearsby and Stuart.

Stuart on the front of Australia's 1995 world championship winning team pursuit outfit with Dean Woods, Rodney McGee and Tim O'Shannessy.

Stuart with his gold medal from the 1993 world championships.

Celebrating the 1995 team pursuit world title with Tim O'Shannessy, Brad McGee and Rod McGee.

Stuart with Cadel Evans after the 2006 world championships in Salzburg.

Stuart wins in the 2003 Australian Championships

Stuart in action during the 2009 road world championships.

Wearing the yellow jersey in the 1998 Tour de France.

Wearing the yellow jersey in the 2001 Tour de France.

At the 2003 Tour de France.

Stuart leading Saxo Bank on stage twenty of the 2009 Tour de France.

Stuart wins the 2004 HEW cyclassics.

On stage seven of the 2012 Tirreno–Adriatico.

Jay Sweet's girlfriend was there and we had a great network of friends.

Anne-Marie was only nineteen when she met Stuart. Funnily enough, she met Stuart's sister Lesley before she met her future husband. 'A good friend of mine had been a podium girl for the first year of the Tour in 1999 and when they needed one more in 2000, she recommended me,' Anne-Marie recalls.

'I had a meeting with Lesley who was working for the Tour Down Under. It was her job to choose the podium girls and we got along great; it was the start of a really good friendship.

'For me, working at the Tour was just a job. I never dreamed I would meet my future husband and have my life turned upside down. I didn't know who Stu was and cycling was only just starting to get the recognition it deserved in Australia.'

In the early days of their relationship, Anne-Marie remembers Stuart 'sweeping me off my feet with his lovable personality and romance'.

'When we had a couple of months apart before I moved to France, he'd send me the most romantic, long emails about how much he missed me, so he does have that soft side to him which not many people see. I fell in love with the Stuart I still love today—his infectious and fun personality, caring and very loving nature. He is so much fun to be around; meeting Stu was the best thing to happen in my life.

'Moving to France was a big decision but it wasn't too scary as I had travelled around Europe the year before. It was an exciting time and I knew I was going into a good support network with Stu. He's such a passionate guy that anything he loves, he puts so much energy into.'

Lesley says she could not be happier that Anne-Marie ended up marrying her brother.

'Anne-Marie and I clicked really quickly from day one. I thought she was a gorgeous girl, really down to earth, fun and honest. We couldn't be happier that he met someone so lovely, so genuine, so beautiful and Australian, which makes it so much easier.'

It wasn't all smooth sailing though. Not long after Anne-Marie arrived in Toulouse, I had to do some motor-pacing and asked her, 'Have you ever ridden a motorbike?' She hadn't but I thought it would be okay because it isn't that hard. I had a 125cc Peugeot and told her to go out the driveway, turn right, sit on 50 km/h and no matter what, don't hit the brakes. 'I'm going to be sitting an inch off the back wheel of the motorbike so if you hit the brakes, I'll end up in hospital,' I told her.

I had a 150 km ride planned and my new motor-pacer

was doing pretty well trying not to look at the Pyrenees
and the sunflowers. Eventually we got to the 75 km turnaround point so I rode past to tell her to follow me into a
cafe for a coffee. But because she'd been concentrating so
hard, as soon as I went past her she must have just switched
off. There was a slight curve at the end of the road and
the next minute I heard the biggest crash behind me. I
turned around to see Anne-Marie had hit the gutter and
gone straight into a wall. The motorbike had been wiped
out and there was blood pouring out of her knees. Straight
away I called an ambulance.

Later, I tried to find my way around the hospital still
holding onto my bike. When I eventually found Anne-
Marie, the doctor told us she'd need double knee surgery
and would spend the next week in hospital. 'Maybe I should
have just started you out with a one-hour motor-pacing
session rather than 150 km,' I said. Anne-Marie didn't find
it funny and has never been near a motorbike since.

Despite that early setback, Anne-Marie stayed with me in
Europe and our relationship grew stronger. Eventually you
reach a point in your life when you decide it's time to grow
up and become responsible. I was always very serious about
my cycling but relationships had been tricky, as they are
for professional athletes. Everyone sees the glamour and
the accolades but they don't read about the tough times or
trying to hold a relationship together when you're living in
different countries. Anne-Marie didn't put massive expec-
tations on me; I guess she didn't know a lot about cycling
or who I was, and that was key.

I'd been thinking about our relationship a lot and one day in June 2001, I was out training with Jay, preparing for the Tour de France, when I told him that I would like to get engaged. Cycling had been such a boys' club for me, which was hard not just for Anne-Marie but for any girl who came along. The boys had always come first, no matter what— my life had been built around a team of blokes since I was sixteen—so this engagement business meant I'd be the first from our group to throw a serious relationship into the mix.

Two days before we were due to leave for the Tour, I realised I hadn't organised a ring, so I told Anne-Marie that I was going into the city to grab a coffee with Jay. We were a couple of experts I can tell you, looking in jewellery stores for an engagement ring. It didn't take long to find what I thought was a pretty decent ring. Jay leaned over my shoulder, took one look at it and said, 'Holy shit, that much for a ring? I'm never getting engaged, these are expensive.'

My initial plan was to propose in Paris after that year's Tour. When I got home I hid the ring in my motorcross boot in the garage and the next day we went to my favourite restaurant, Le Palmiers, before I left for the Tour. We were sitting there drinking champagne when Anne-Marie must have sensed something was up because she asked, 'Are you okay?' My mind was on the whole proposal gig but I said, 'Yeah, I'm fine.' As I looked around at this perfect summer's night, on the river, eating my favourite entrée foie gras, it struck me: this is the moment, I've got to do it now. So right then and there I asked Anne-Marie to marry me, even though I didn't have the ring with us.

After we finished dinner, I raced home and grabbed the ring out of my motorcross boot, then started calling everyone back home.

As soon as the old man found out we were engaged, he started building a deck out the front of our place at Ingle Farm. He reckoned if I was going to be home with my groomsmen the night before I tied the knot, we needed a deck. Besides, he'd been talking about building it for twenty years so my engagement was the kick-start he needed.

As it turned out, the deck came in pretty handy the night before the wedding when I plucked about ten bottles of my finest red wine from the cellar and sat with the boys to toast the occasion. We were married on a 42-degree day in Adelaide on 23 November 2002. Anne-Marie did a lot of work organising everything; all I had to do was take care of the cars, which were Daimlers. Jay was best man and my other groomsmen were my brother Darren, Nathan Rattley, Leigh Bryan and Paul Neighbour.

Nathan, one of my oldest friends, was still living in the same house at Ingle Farm where we grew up together. He was the first person I ran to see when I got back from Barcelona with my Olympic silver medal because we did everything together. Leigh had become my long-time trainer and personal coach but also one of my best friends, and Paul Neighbour literally is my neighbour in Unley where I live when I'm in Adelaide. He's a successful businessman and has been my go-to man for advice; I even bought my house from him.

Rattley is not a competitive rider and is far from a cycling fanatic, which means he and Stuart share a unique friendship outside the bubble of the sport. He says Stuart has been there for him and vice versa through the good times and bad. None more so than in 1993 when Rattley lost his mother to cancer.

'Stuey was pretty close with her, and Mum adored him,' Rattley says. 'He'd be over for dinner most nights if he could, he especially loved her curries.'

'But in 1993 Mum was not well and Stuey could see I was struggling. And this is the character of the bloke: in the middle of training and racing he just dropped everything and said, "Let's go camping." It was a really emotional time.

'When we came home from the camping trip Mum was in a coma. I was nineteen at the time and there was only Mum, me and my sister. Stuey stood with me when the ambulance left, he came to hospital with me where I was emotionally messed up, and he was pretty shattered as well.'

The two have an unbreakable bond, even though they only see each other a few times a year. Stuart is the godfather of Rattley's eldest child, Jemmah. 'I've seen him do some amazing things in his cycling career, but his character and his loyalty will always outshine anything he's ever done on the bike,' Rattley says. 'We have both had our fair share of adversity over the years and it's because of our close friendship that we have been able to turn to one another in those times.'

Another friend who has become like family to Stuart is his long-time manager and friend, Max Stevens. The pair have worked together for the best part of twenty years and while Stuart does most of his own contact negotiations, Stevens takes care of the rest including sponsorship, appearances and organising his schedule in Australia.

Stevens remembers meeting Stuart as an eighteen-year-old over lunch with mutual friend Gary Niewand in Adelaide. 'I was a football reporter with Channel 7 and a very keen cyclist, so I started to watch Stuart's career with great interest,' Stevens recalls. 'I was in the right spot at the right time and became Stuey's manager.

'While I have the greatest respect for everyone I've managed over the years, being involved with an internationally revered athlete is another level. Over the journey I've tried hard to become the "manager" as opposed to the "friend" but Stuart is such an infectious person, you just can't help but fall back into that mate-relationship. Stuey has given so much to his sport, his family and the people around him.'

Stevens says his relationship with Stuart also opened many doors. 'I remember walking up to Fabian Cancellara at the world championships one year and asking for a photo. At first he was quite unapproachable but when I explained my friendship with Stuart, Fabian was instantly happy to talk to me. That's Stuey's influence; it's like having an open visa to meeting the movers and shakers of international cycling.'

Stevens admires Stuart's loyalty and passion for the sport. 'Every deal we've cut, every contract, Stuart has always put money back into junior cycling in South Australia. He is a class act.'

John Trevorrow is a multiple national champion who used to compete against Stuart's father Brian. He first took serious notice of Stuart at the 1993 track world titles. 'You could see everyone was nervous before the race and Stuey just said to them, "We can't lose this," and he was right,' he recalls.

Trevorrow has been at almost every one of Stuart's Tours de France and witnessed it all, from stage victories to life-threatening crashes. But he said Stuart's 2007 Paris–Roubaix victory would be etched in his memory forever. 'It's the only bike race I've ever put on TV and watched three or four times; it's like a favourite movie,' he says.

But what impresses him most about Stuart is his character. On the morning of the 2013 Paris–Roubaix, Trevorrow received a text message from Stuart who had learned he (Trevorrow) had been diagnosed with cancer. That Stuart took the time to send the message on the morning of Paris–Roubaix meant the world to Trevorrow.

Anne-Marie and I invited about two hundred people to our wedding. The ceremony was in a small church in North Adelaide and the reception at Town Hall. In between we sent everyone to the Botanic Gardens where there was a marquee and a ridiculous amount of alcohol. Because it was 40 degrees everyone went pretty hard so I'm not sure whether half the people remember the wedding, but it was a fantastic night.

Being the wife of a professional cyclist has got to be one of the toughest gigs on the planet. Guys who play football, soccer or tennis—they're in stadiums, the wives can come to watch and it might be one night away at a time for an away game. But bike-riders can spend more than two hundred days a year on the road. On top of that, we're very demanding, we're constantly complaining about training hard, we're tired, and walking was my number one hate. I would get home from training and Anne-Marie would say, 'Do you want to go to the shops or to the city?' and I'd be too stuffed and just want to chill out and recover. As athletes, we can be extremely selfish and anyone who says otherwise is lying. I think that goes across every top-level sport in the world because you have to be selfish if you want to succeed.

During my career I had two different lifestyles. There was

the Stuart who lived in Europe for ten months of the year, was professional, trained his arse off and was hardly home; and there was the Stuart who spent two months in Australia and was relaxed, went to barbecues, had a few beers and did a lot of socialising with our friends and family. That was Anne-Marie's time because I realised the sacrifices she made for me the other ten months of the year.

Anne-Marie never asked me to give up cycling. I asked her the question quite a few times, especially after a few big crashes when I managed to put myself in some pretty bad situations. Is enough enough? Should I just stop? But each time she said, 'It's up to you, you're the one suffering on the bike, you're the one who has to leave your family.' I even asked my son Seth a few times whether I should quit. It happened as recently as the end of 2012 when my uncle Syd Jacobs passed away. I was 39 years old, my kids were in a foreign country, it was the end of a long, long year, I'd come back from another big crash and two weeks in hospital with broken bones, and I'd never felt so isolated from my family in my whole life. I came home and said, 'Seth, do you want Daddy to race anymore?' And if he'd said, 'Yes Daddy, can you please stop racing,' I would have packed up. But each time I asked Seth he said, 'No way, then I couldn't go on the team bus and who would I watch in the races?'

Anne-Marie says spending half her life overseas away from her immediate family had its moments, but the positive experiences far outweighed the difficult times. 'The experience of being around cycling in the early years was incredible. I had a lot to learn about bike-racing and going to my first Tour de France and first Olympics was so eye-opening and so memorable,' she says.

'Cycling would consume a lot of our private life but mostly in a good way. I chose to be a part of this lifestyle and become Stuart's number-one support, knowing the challenges that come with it. Everything we planned throughout the year was based around him and his job but that's not a problem, that's how it has been from the start and I now share the same passion for cycling that he does.

'Stu has so much time for all the people he meets and this can sometimes jeopardise the time I have with him but it's one of the many qualities that shape the incredible person he is. Yes, there were times when it was hard and lonely but I have been lucky to have such a great support network among my friends both in Australia and abroad. My family has been a huge support and they too have developed a love for cycling, sharing the excitement of Stu's career.'

Stuart's sister Lesley says one of the most challenging things about Stuart's career was that for the most part, his immediate family could only watch it unfold from afar. 'We couldn't afford to follow him around every year, so we had to watch whatever media coverage we could.'

It wasn't until a trip to Europe in 2001 that Lesley realised the big brother who used to boss her around, and with whom she would spend endless hours in summer watching cricket on television, had become a big deal in world cycling.

'When I went on a holiday to Europe I saw him at the start line of the Tour of Flanders and yelled out, "Stu, Stu!" and ran across and gave him a big hug. Then, as I turned around, I realised there were people everywhere, two and three deep in a circle around him. It was such an eye-opening moment when I realised just how big he is over there and also how big the sport of cycling is.'

The 2012 season was the first time I took Seth for a proper ride and he loved it. He's obsessed with cycling, which I'm trying to steer him away from and into soccer. I'll wake up in the morning and he's out riding in the street, practising victory salutes in the rain. But I don't want him to be obsessed with cycling because I loved so many sports as a kid. I'm afraid he'll pick cycling and that'll be it; I want him to get out there and try everything as well.

During my career I was aware there were guys who wouldn't fight for a spot on the wheel in the final of a sprint because they had a young family at home—and that's exactly what happened to me. One of the reasons I started shying away from bunch sprinting was because it's mad dangerous, and as soon as you have a kid you start seeing poles and parked cars and cliffs that go hundreds of metres to the bottom. Having a family makes you look at things from a different perspective.

However, that fear didn't go through my mind when I was descending a climb because I tried to block it out. I love descending, I know Jensie thinks I'm mad but I am in full control and there's a real art to downhill racing. I love plummeting down a mountain when you've got the whole road to yourself; it's like downhill skiing, and if you watch the best guys like Thor Hushovd and Fabian Cancellara, they attack the corners like a slalom.

I've been lucky enough to have three beautiful, healthy kids. Seth was born in 2003, Keira in 2007 and Tayla in 2009. When I had my big crash in the 2007 Tour de France, Anne-Marie was eight-and-a-half months pregnant with Keira and drove six hours from Monaco to see me in intensive care. I only just made it out of hospital in time to see Keira born, then missed Tayla's birth on 6 September because I was at the Vuelta a España preparing for the world championships. That was one of the most difficult things I've had to do, and I'll never forget getting the phone call with the news in the middle of the night, which was the end of sleep for me. I went to breakfast with the biggest grin on my face but at the same time I was pretty down because I wanted to be there so badly. It got harder and harder as the days went on, and after two-and-a-half weeks I cracked and said, 'Look, I've just got to go home because I can't concentrate on riding.'

Being a dad is incredible and the first time you hold your

kid in your arms is unbelievable, it's beyond magical. When Seth was born I was running around hugging strangers in the hospital, I was that proud—in fact, I was so excited I went to a Powderfinger concert to celebrate! I'd better explain how that happened.

Powderfinger is one of my favourite bands, and in 2001 I went to their concert in Cologne, Germany, with Corey Sweet and Luke Roberts. It was a pretty intimate show, we met the guys and got to take beers up to them on stage. From that night I kept in touch with them, mainly bass guitarist John Collins, who is better known as JC.

I happened to be in Adelaide when they came to perform. I organised to play golf with them at Grange during the day then go to their concert that night, although the timing wasn't great because Anne-Marie was heavily pregnant with Seth.

Sure enough, at 1 am Anne-Marie woke up with contractions and as we drove into Burnside Hospital, despite being that excited about the birth of my first child, I was nevertheless thinking, 'I'm going to have to miss golf with the boys!'—it's funny how the male mind works. Seth's birth was amazing and I stayed at the hospital with Anne-Marie until 8 pm when she started getting pretty tired. As I was driving home I stopped and bought a bottle of champagne and a cigar—even though I hate smoking. I wanted to celebrate becoming a father in style. I got a heap of messages from my mates asking whether I was still going to the Powderfinger concert but I said I was just happy to go home and reflect on such an awesome day.

Yet sitting in my courtyard in Unley, still on my own, the boys eventually cracked me. In the end it was a message from JC who said it was unfortunate I couldn't be there but he understood. Stuff it, I thought, Anne-Marie was asleep anyway and I was home on my own, so at the last minute I decided to go to the concert, letting all the boys know I was on my way.

I'm pretty happy I went because Powderfinger dedicated a song to Anne-Marie and to Seth—'My Happiness' which still gives me goosebumps every time I hear it.

I remember Seth going to his first Tour de France, and when I won the Olympics in 2004 Anne-Marie and Seth made a special trip to Athens for the race. Knowing my wife and baby boy were in the velodrome, I definitely rode above and beyond myself that night. They were there when I won Paris–Roubaix; I knew they were standing at the finish in the velodrome and I wanted to make them proud. Riding in you would have seen me rubbing my belly because Anne-Marie was pregnant with Keira but I think I did about fifteen different victory salutes all rolled into one. Even having the kids at the Tour Down Under was awesome. Looking over, seeing them in your team's jersey screaming, 'Go Daddy!' was an amazing feeling. All three of them were at the London Olympics in 2012 with their faces painted in the Australian colours and I was so proud.

Stuart's career has had a big impact on Seth, who joined a cycling club in Luxembourg, where the family had moved. There's a photo of Seth, aged eight months, chewing on Stuart's gold medal from the 2004 Olympics, and his love for the sport has grown ever since.

'I've got a Scott bike, yellow, black and white, and I've got the GreenEDGE top,' nine-year-old Seth says. 'And the Australian one from the 2012 Olympics pretty much fits me. I've done a 30 km ride with Dad. We rode into town which was 15 km and that meant another 15 km back. I do cricket and tennis but cycling is my favourite sport.'

When he's not riding his bike with Stuart, Seth says their favourite activity is playing chess. And what was his advice for his dad before he would leave for a race?

'I just tell him I'll miss him a lot,' Seth says.

As much as Seth loved watching his dad race, Stuart's father Brian was just as passionate about his son's career. The three generations shared a special moment in March 2013 when they took the Orica-GreenEDGE team car on a reconnaissance mission over the cobblestones in the days leading up to the Tour of Flanders.

Brian says Stuart's career took him to the inner sanctum of

world cycling and delivered some privileged experiences. He remembers shedding a tear when Stuart told him he would be flown to Europe to watch the 1999 Tour de France thanks to a sponsorship deal. 'An all-expenses-paid trip for two people to the Tour de France was like striking the lottery,' Brian recalls.

In later years they would watch the Tour—as well as all the Classics—unfold from the comfort of their loungeroom, even if it meant sitting up until 2am.

'That caravan,' Brian says, pointing to the green-and-white-striped caravan in his backyard at Ingle Farm, 'I bought it so I could tour around Australia in my mid-fifties when I retired. But it hasn't been off the bloody blocks!'

What happened?

'Stuey's career happened! I've seen 99.9 per cent of France and hardly any of Australia,' Brian says.

CHAPTER 7

YELLOW, GREEN AND GUTTED

The 2001 season remains one of the biggest and most successful years of my career but it was also an emotional rollercoaster.

The year couldn't have started any better when I won my second Tour Down Under. I arrived in Adelaide still pretty frustrated about finishing second in the race the year before by just twelve seconds, and I was determined to make amends. My preparation was perfect and knowing the race was likely to be decided by time bonuses, I attacked at every opportunity on the road.

The key to winning the Tour Down Under in those days was consistency—finishing at the front every day—and I started with two second placings before taking the race lead on Stage 3 from McLaren Vale to Victor Harbor. The lead changed a couple more times throughout the week but I was consistent enough to win my second TDU title by two seconds without actually winning a stage. The 1999 TDU victory was a bit of a surprise but the following year, guys were coming to Australia better trained and better prepared. So winning in 2001 was pretty cool because the stakes had been raised.

Throughout the European spring I was focused on trying to win the green jersey at the Tour de France. In previous years I seemed to stumble across it because I'd been so aggressive, but it had now become my single big ambition for the year. Things got a bit interesting, however, when my teammate Thor Hushovd won the Tour of Sweden, a lead-up race to the Tour de France, and I finished second. The night before the Tour de France prologue in Dunkirk, Roger Legeay called Thor and me into his hotel room for a meeting. It seemed a bit strange because normally we'd meet as an entire team, but this night he looked at me and said, 'Stuey, what is your ambition for the race?' I replied, 'What do you mean, I want to try to win the green jersey.' Then he looked at Thor who said, 'Well, I want to have a go at the green jersey.' I was stunned, because although Thor's sprints were coming along well, I didn't expect this. So I said, 'Mate, it's hard enough trying to win the green jersey with your whole team helping you, let alone having one of your teammates wanting to have a go as well.' It was a really tricky situation because I'm great friends with Thor but I just didn't see it coming. Okay, I hadn't won the green jersey before but I'd finished second a couple of times. So Roger said to us, 'Well, whoever gets the best position in the prologue, the team works for them.'

So my hopes of winning the green jersey rested on the next day's 8.2 km prologue. It was as if a switch went off in my head because I was like, 'Right, I'm going to show you.' And I did because I had a cracker of a prologue. Christophe Moreau won the day but it was the best prologue of my life as I finished eighth, 13 seconds behind him, while Thor also had a great ride and was nineteenth at 17 seconds. I was only four years older than Thor but it was like the old bloke having to stamp his authority over the youngster. I couldn't have my teammates coming into a sprint of the Tour de France wondering which one of us they were meant to be working for and, to Thor's credit, he was happy with that once it was settled in the prologue.

From that day, I had one of the most amazing Tours. The rollercoaster ride truly began on Stage 2 from Saint-Omer to Antwerp. I was in a breakaway with about fifteen riders and looked like taking the yellow jersey if we survived, but coming to the finish it all went to shit. It felt like the whole breakaway was against me; whether or not that was true I'll never know, but the feeling I got was very negative. Marc Wauters was the only guy in the break who I couldn't afford to let win the stage because he was my only threat for the overall lead. But as so often happens in cycling, it all went pear-shaped. Wauters escaped in the final few hundred metres and won the stage while I finished a frustrating fifth with the same time but Wauters was in yellow. To make matters worse, the winner of the stage was to get a $25,000 diamond and be congratulated by the King of Belgium.

I went back to the team bus and when Roger came to see me I was gutted, I was absolutely distraught, because I did everything close to perfect but it wasn't enough. I basically broke down and thought, 'That's it, there goes the yellow jersey,' because Wauters was a good enough climber to hold on for the next few days—or so I thought. Roger being Roger, he hung out with me for a while but I was still pretty devastated at the dinner table because I felt I'd let the boys down after they'd worked so hard to put me in the best position.

With my focus on targeting the green jersey, I did fairly minimal training in the mountains and heaps of motor-pacing and sessions on the home-trainer smashing myself in the sprints. But I've never been a pure sprinter, which I said from day one. I never had the power of Mark Cavendish or Mario Cipollini, and I didn't have the speed of Robbie McEwen.

Robbie is one of the fastest, most powerful accelerators the planet has ever seen. Guys like Cipollini need five or six guys in front of them for the last 4 to 5 km but Robbie would be on his own, battling it out then pop out of nowhere and blitz everyone; I never had anything like that. My strength in sprinting was to position myself where I wanted because

I was strong enough to do repetitive efforts before the actual sprint. If I was badly placed I could do one sprint and be back in position.

I'd deliberately pick on guys who I knew were married and had a young family because they weren't prepared to fight. You'd ride up and basically lean on them with a bit of an elbow to push them off the wheel. You're not out to crash anyone, but I'd see Jan Svorada, for example, sitting behind Erik Zabel and I knew Svorada had a kid and was happily married, so that was his weakness. I knew he wouldn't fight for the wheel so I'd go next to him, lean on him and get him out of the way. I learnt a lot about how to handle a bike from my track racing and it was all fair, it was part of the race, and I have been on the receiving end of plenty. Zabel, however, was a real fighter and I worked that out early on. I'd give him a bit of a push and he'd smack me back; we had some real ding-dong battles and he would never let the wheel go.

My other strength was that I could still sprint at the same speed after 300 km as I could after 30 km. The longer the race, the better as far as I was concerned. I could maintain my speed through the hundreds of thousands of kilometres of endurance track training I did when I was younger, whereas for a lot of the pure sprinters, their top speed comes down after 200 or 220 km. I never won a bunch sprint in the Tour, I had about twenty second places, but my forte was being consistently up there and still hanging in there on the medium mountains, which is how I could fight for the green jersey.

Once the disappointment of missing the yellow jersey by twelve seconds had subsided in the 2001 Tour, I focused on Stage 3 from Antwerp to Seraing as a new opportunity. When the climbs started coming in towards the end of the stage, I was still angry at myself for what had happened the day before, but then I heard over the team radio that Wauters in the yellow jersey was being dropped. My ears suddenly pricked up. If that was correct, all I had to do was hang in there with the front group and I'd be in yellow that night. There were only sixty guys in the front as a wave of emotion came over me and I found another gear. Roger was on the radio saying, 'Hang in there, hang in there.' Obviously I was right in contention for the green jersey, which was meant to be my priority, but you try worrying about green when there's yellow on the line!

Zabel won the stage and I crossed the line with the front group, an emotional wreck. The day before I'd seen my yellow jersey dreams go down the drain, but here I was the following day, about to step on the podium and pull it on; it was a massive moment. I didn't give a crap about the stage or not being up there for the sprint. I'd been in an impossible situation but I'd managed to come out of it and get the yellow jersey.

When I crossed the finish line I collapsed on my bike and got pretty emotional. I was so relieved and so proud to be standing on the podium and pulling on the jersey. It was a very different situation to 1998; it was like a different sport. The 2001 Tour de France was a dream, confirming for me that if you strive for something, if you sacrifice and put in the hard yards, anything is possible.

Cruelly, with the benefit of hindsight, I know that I should have contested the sprint that day. That year I lost the green jersey in Paris on the last day of the Tour by just eight points. I only had to do half a sprint that day and finish tenth or fifteenth, not thirtieth, and I could have won the green jersey. Losing green to Zabel is one of the biggest disappointments of my career. But at the same time I did wear the yellow jersey and I'm not sure I'd trade that for anything either.

I was still pinching myself as I started Stage 4 from Hay to Verdun in yellow, with a 17-second lead over Christophe Moreau. A break went up the road but it was contained and I eventually finished in the front group to protect my lead in what was a surprisingly stress-free day as the leader of the biggest race in the world.

I wasn't so sure, however, that I'd still have the jersey the next day as Stage 5 was a 67 km team time-trial that threatened to stretch our Crédit Agricole team to the limit. We'd never won a team time-trial and were up against the supersquads of the Discovery Channel, ONCE, Rabobank—all these teams with time-trial experts. I was pretty certain I was going to lose the jersey.

We were a team of foreigners in a French team but we were good. There was Jens Voigt, Thor Hushovd, Bobby Julich, Jonathan Vaughters and me, then a bunch of pretty good French bike-riders who were good guys but no superstars or stage winners, just helpers. On paper we definitely weren't the strongest team in the Tour de France.

The morning of the team time-trial, it was cold and wet when we went out training. I was suffering because I'd been doing sprints and had gone really deep in the prologue, so I was already fatigued. I even wore the yellow jersey out training because when you've got it, you wear it for every minute you can. Just before we rolled off the ramp I started getting into the boys saying, 'Come on guys, let's just get it up and going and see what happens,' because everyone was really nervous and I was probably the most nervous of all. By the time we started it was pouring rain and riders were sitting an inch off the wheel in front of them with water squirting up in their face—I could hardly see and my heart was in my mouth the whole time.

A team time-trial on the road is a lot like a team pursuit on the track—only with more riders. Each does a turn on the front then swings out of the way and joins the back of the queue. When it's working, it's beautiful to watch even though it doesn't feel like that as a rider.

From the first kilometre, the lactate kicked in and five days into a Tour de France, it hurt. You're just concentrating so much on breathing, getting the oxygen in, the lactic acid out, using your lung capacity and relaxing your arms. It was then I looked down and we were sitting on 55 km/h in the pouring rain and I was thinking, 'We're going pretty quick here.' At the first time check we were about twelve seconds in front and I was in shock. But I reckoned we'd blow up soon because it was a 67 km team time-trial and that's bloody long.

After 15 km we lost one guy to a puncture. He was the

strongest French rider we had, but we didn't even flinch. Then, soon after, one more French guy couldn't come to the front anymore so we were basically down to the five of us with one French guy coming through every now and then; nevertheless, we were absolutely motoring along. We had our ear-pieces in and Roger didn't miss a beat. When you do your turn on the front, you swing off, ease up a bit, the rest of the team comes past and you have to get back on in last position. This can be the hardest part because you've got to swing on at the exact moment otherwise you lose the wheel, you're out of the slipstream and you have to fight like hell to catch up.

After a few of those efforts you never recover but Roger, to his credit that day, did not miss one rider. He'd call out, 'Stuey now!' and without even looking you'd just swing left and would be parked smack bang on the wheel and get to recover as much as possible before it was your turn again.

As we approached the second time check, I thought, 'Right, this is the one, it's come down surely,' but our lead had increased, it had basically doubled! That was the first time I thought, 'Holy crap, we could pull this off.' Roger was screaming in the radio and every time I'd swing off after my turn I'd say, 'Come on guys, we can do this.' And every time I started hurting, I'd look down and see the yellow sleeves on my jersey and think, 'I'm wearing the yellow jersey in the Tour de France, and we're leading the team time-trial.' I think the jersey gave everyone that 10 per cent extra that day, it gave us an edge. Whether it's the pink jersey in the Giro d'Italia or the ochre jersey in the

Tour Down Under: you go deeper and harder than what you think you can, and that day the whole team rose to the occasion.

The last 5 km Roger was screaming at me not to do any more turns because the stage finished up a little climb and he was worried that I'd get dropped and lose the jersey. So the last 5 km I had to sit on, which is not my style, but I remember Thor being on the front for the last couple of kilometres and he was absolutely stomping which meant the world to me.

Everyone was incredible that day; we won by 31 seconds over ONCE and 54 seconds over Festina. I'll never, ever forget standing on the podium with all my teammates, wearing yellow. It was definitely one of the proudest moments of my career. It's one thing to cross the finish line and take the win for yourself, but to do it with your teammates moves it to the next level; to have everyone so committed and working to keep me in the yellow jersey. I've never played football but I guess that's what it might feel like to win a final.

It was a momentous day for our Crédit Agricole team when Stage 6 began in Commercy. We held the top three places in the general classification with me, Jens and Bobby, thanks to our efforts in the previous day's team time-trial. I was in the yellow jersey and led by 26 seconds to Jens and by 27 seconds to Bobby. We faced a 211.5 km day to Strasbourg which we anticipated would finish with a bunch sprint so all we had to do was control any dangerous breaks.

As expected, a break eventually got away but never posed

a threat to my overall lead as my teammates worked hard on the front of the peloton to bring the race back together. I contested the sprint but because I was wearing the yellow jersey I was only semi-committed; the last thing I wanted to do was crash. So I'd fight a bit for position but I was more worried about keeping the bike upright than anything so I shadowed Zabel in the final as he finished one spot ahead of me in fourth place. Once again, if I knew what would happen in Paris on the final day, I might have gone a bit harder. But hindsight is a wonderful thing!

The next day was a bit more interesting with Stage 7 from Strasbourg to Colmar presenting a few testing climbs. It wasn't classified as a mountains day but it was a really hard, nasty day. Jens, being the attacking animal that he is, jumped into the first break of the day to take the heat off our team having to work again because I wasn't confident about staying on the front of the bunch all day. We went up the front to make it look like we were going to protect the jersey, but then let the break go and eventually it stayed away. That night I handed the yellow jersey to Jens as he turned a 26-second deficit into a 2:34 lead while I'd suddenly slipped to third place, 4:03 behind. I remember racing along, aware that I was going to lose the jersey which was disappointing, but also knowing that Jens was going to get it. And if anyone in the world deserved the yellow jersey, Jens did, so the disappointment didn't last long. He is the biggest workhorse and probably the best teammate I've ever had in my career, he's just an animal, he's all about the team.

The following stage was one of the most bizarre days in Tour de France history. It was pouring rain and freezing cold as we started Stage 8 in Colmar. Our tactic was to defend the jersey, but if I was up the road in a breakaway the team wasn't going to chase. One of the Rabobank guys came up to me on the start line and said, 'I bet you're going to be wearing yellow again tonight.' To be honest, it hadn't crossed my mind because I was four minutes behind, so I looked at him and said, 'Yeah whatever,' as we rolled off in the pissing-down rain.

Next thing I know, I'm in a breakaway with thirteen others and the lead started climbing—one minute, two minutes, three minutes, four minutes. I was the best-placed rider in the break on general classification so I knew that my team wouldn't be chasing and it seemed all the other teams were thinking the same thing—the weather was so crap and the breakaway was so big. In the end we finished 36 minutes ahead of the bunch and put the entire peloton out of the time limit. If they'd stuck to the rules, the next day there would have only been fourteen of us starting the Tour de France. But the commissaires changed the ruling. The cut-off on a flat stage is normally 20 per cent of the winner's time but they said due to the shocking conditions they'd re-assess the classification. It was so cold that as we came to the finish, guys were attacking and I couldn't even change my gears. My hands were frozen and I couldn't put my brakes on, I had to put my wrist around my brake lever and pull my arm back to slow down. So I was stuck in the one gear as Erik Dekker won the stage and I finished a couple of minutes back—but it was good enough for me to regain the yellow jersey. Even better, I had the green jersey as well after collecting enough points up the road to take it from Zabel.

Yellow obviously trumps green so that's the jersey I wore the following day because I led the race by four minutes, but to me the big bonus was my lead in the points classification. Yellow was awesome but those points in the green jersey became really valuable as I now led by thirteen points.

While Zabel was so calculating and precise with where he'd get points every day, I'd just rock up and be in a breakaway on a mountain day, which he hated. One day he called me a mad dog, but in a good way. He said, 'I never know what you're going to do.' In later years, I decided to have a lot of fun with him because I'd attack in the most random places. I'd realise he was following me, sitting on my wheel from the start line, so I'd make out that I had to stop for a toilet break, pull off the road, take my foot out of the pedal then click back in and ride off. My other trick was to go on the other side of the bunch and I'd see him arching his neck looking around trying to find me. I was just trying to get into his head and mess with him because he was quicker than me, and we both knew it. So I had to think of other ways to beat him.

The mind games were still going as we approached the final stage of the Tour in Paris. I held the green jersey by just two points over Zabel and I remember saying, 'Oh come on Erik, please let me win, man, you've won five or six—and it's my birthday.' So he said, 'Really, it's your birthday?' And I couldn't keep a straight face. 'No, shit no, but come on.' Even if I went along with the joke I still don't think he would have let me win.

Although we were fierce opponents, we still had plenty of fun together. Zabel was probably the most controlled, level-headed sprinter I've ever seen. He never did any stupid moves—obviously he'd fight you for the wheel and if he had a good position he wouldn't let it go—but he never caused an accident or threw a hook at you in the sprint. He won four Milan–San Remos, so he had an incredible career. I just happened to be competing against the best green jersey sprinter the Tour de France has ever seen.

From the moment I took the green jersey on Stage 8 the battle with Zabel was intense. Every bonus sprint was like racing for a stage win and we followed each other like you would not believe. I wouldn't let him out of my sight and if I tried any sneaky little tricks like attacking on a mountain day, he'd be right behind me. I'd think, 'Beautiful, let's go Erik,' because I knew that it would wear him out. I would attack randomly, try to get into breaks and make him work as well because that was my only way of trying to beat him.

Our battle continued for the next twelve days and I managed to keep my nose in front while the race for the yellow jersey was happening miles ahead of us in the mountains. On Stage 16 from Castelsarrasin to Sarran, Zabel was eighth and I was ninth. On Stage 17 from Brive-la-Gaillarde to Montlucon, he was sixth and I was seventh, and by Stage 19 it all came to a head.

We faced 149.5 km from Orléans to Evry on the

penultimate stage before our sprint into Paris. On the team bus before the stage we spoke about what would happen if I had a mishap in the last couple of kilometres because the green jersey could be gone in the blink of an eye. So I said, 'Which of you is 177 cm tall? One of you guys has got to be close to that.' One of them said, 'I'm 180 cm,' so my instructions to him were to follow me in the sprint and if I had any dramas in the run to the final, he was to give me a bike.

As fate would have it, with 3 km to go, my rear derailleur exploded when someone hit it with their front wheel. Thank God my teammate saw what happened because we both came to a skidding stop at 60 km/h. I ripped his bike from under his legs and because the seat was 3 cm too high, I rode to the finish out of the saddle in the sprinting position. I had to put in a massive effort to get back near the front from the team cars, but I still couldn't sit down so coming to the finish I was that angry that I pulled a crazy sprint. Romans Vainsteins was the world champion and I banged him out of the way with a big head-butt, opened up a gap and Zabel was right there, I had him in my sights. By that point I simply could not go any faster and, despite throwing the kitchen sink at him, he won the stage and I was second. It was probably one of the best sprints I'd ever done, coming from so far back, my best second place ever, and I'd saved the day because I still had the green jersey.

I remember saying to Zabel after the race, 'Man, I wish I had my own bike.' He just looked at me and shook his head in disbelief. He couldn't fathom that I'd had to change my bike with a few kilometres to go. 'You are bloody unbeliev-able, what have I got to do to beat you?' he said.

I barely slept that night knowing that if I could hang on and somehow beat him in Paris on the final stage, I would win my first ever green jersey. I led by just two points and we had a plan but I was pretty nervous. It basically came down to whoever finished ahead would win—and I hadn't beaten Zabel in a sprint because he was the best sprinter in the world.

As we came into Paris it seemed like the whole peloton was relaxed. Lance Armstrong was drinking champagne on his bike but I was experiencing the most stressful moment of my entire career. Not only did I have to win the last sprint, but I had two intermediate sprints on the road, which no one else gave a shit about because they were already in Paris; as far as they were concerned, they were finished.

With Zabel two points behind me, we decided to send big Jens and another teammate up the road to take the intermediate points away from him. That was my only real hope because I wasn't going to beat Zabel man-on-man at the finish, I had to be realistic. So Jens attacked 3 km before the intermediate sprint but Telekom was one of the most experienced teams in the world, Zabel had won the green jersey five years in a row and he wasn't going to be done by some silly little tactic like that. So Telekom took over, brought Jens back and stuffed me around, which was the first time I'd been on the receiving end of some of those tactics.

Approaching the first intermediate sprint, three Telekom guys led Zabel out and I was right behind him in fifth place. But while I was waiting for him to sprint, he just let the wheel go and two of his teammates in front were away before I even realised what was going on. He played the master trick on me by letting his own teammates ride off, then he sprinted across to them and they'd stop at the last second, letting him win. When I realised what was happening I launched but by then Zabel had won, Vinokourov got second and I was third so still got a point. 'You dirty bastard,' I thought, 'that was a good trick!' At least now I knew their plan, so it was, 'Okay pal, the gloves are off.'

When they tried it on the next sprint, Zabel still beat me but I was second so as we rode onto the Champs Elysées I had to finish ahead of him. If I was tenth, he had to be eleventh, and if I won he had to finish second, there were no ifs or buts about it. I thought my best chance was to come past him on the cobbles because it's quite a difficult sprint on the Champs Elysées. At one stage I thought, 'Why don't I dive-bomb underneath him and whack him into the barriers'— I'm not going to lie and say these thoughts weren't going through my head. So we went hammer and tongs the whole way down the Champs Elysées and I couldn't get him.

Zabel didn't win the stage, Jan Svorada did, but Zabel was second and I was third. Even though in the back of my mind I always knew this was the likely outcome, I was absolutely devastated. I didn't even want to go back to the team truck so I just rode down the Champs Elysées on my own for a while. I was gutted beyond belief to wear the green jersey for eighteen stages and lose it on the last sprint by a wheel length.

As I would later learn, Zabel admitted to doping throughout his career. That was a tough one for me to take because of course I'm disappointed I never won the green jersey; but at the same time, there's nothing I can do about it. People would be within their rights to turn around to me and say, 'Hang on, you were standing on the podium in 1998 wearing yellow and taking someone else's spot, knowing you'd used EPO.' There were other riders who kicked our arses in the Classics, not just in the Tour, while not racing clean, and sure, it's frustrating. But saying, 'I should have been third that year' or whatever, wouldn't achieve anything.

The disappointment of losing green aside, we had a big celebration in Paris that night because it was still a magical Tour for all of us. As far as years go, 2001 is right up there with 2004 and Paris–Roubaix in 2007. They're what I call my 'Penfolds Grange years'—and as Australian wine-lovers know, you don't pop the cork on those very often.

CHAPTER 8

WORK HARD, PLAY HARD

Throughout my career I was always good at managing the lifestyle of an elite athlete but at the same time trying to be as normal as possible—even though 'normal' isn't really the right word to describe my life.

Being a junior athlete at international level, then leaving Australia to move to Europe at such a young age, meant I didn't have the typical teenage/early twenties experiences of summer holidays, barbecues, parties, eighteenths and twenty-firsts. I'm not for one minute complaining—I chose this pathway and I wouldn't change it for a second—but there are certain things you miss out on. On my twenty-first birthday, I did 10 x 4 km and 10 x 2 km efforts on the track with Charlie Walsh holding a stopwatch and screaming at me.

As professional cyclists, we're basically trained animals because pushing ourselves to suffer through pain is all we know and it's what we do best. With all due respect to other sports, we don't stand around a stadium playing with a ball; we go out on the roads and bloody hurt ourselves and if you're not hurting yourself, you're not achieving anything. So at times during my career, mostly in the early years, I'd go out on a 200 km training ride, hurt myself, get home and crack open a few cold beers. It was part and parcel of the lifestyle of being a young bloke living the dream in Europe.

In the early years of Stuart's career he and Jens Voigt became close friends and shared many good times together, including in Toulouse where Stuart lived along with fellow Aussies Henk Vogels and Jay Sweet.

Voigt says he had to grow up fast when he met his new Australian friends. The three of them ate breakfast together, went training together and grocery shopping which normally ended up being sidetracked by a few beers.

According to Voigt, by the 1990s Stuart could drink more on a night out than just about anyone who cared to join him, despite weighing no more than 70 kg. Voigt says he learned very quickly that it was not smart to go beer for beer with him. 'People who tried, they just went down,' he remarks.

'But Stuey, he knows, "Okay, I've got to turn the switch now, be professional, train hard"—and he's there.'

Voigt remembers one particular morning turning up at Stuart's house for training after a night out. 'So I show up there at 9 am and you could see Jay and Stuey were suffering but they were dressed and ready to go; then they attacked in the big ring out the driveway. I was like, "Oh, we are in for a shit day here," because they dared each other. That day we trained for five hours with intervals on the climbs at full gas. I said, "Hey, coffee stop maybe? Half-time break?" But they just wanted to get it done. They lived up to the idea that if you can party, you can also work.'

There is, however, a serious side to Voigt when he talks about his long-time Aussie teammate. 'He is—and this is a pure, honest compliment straight from my heart—a freak of nature, in every sense of the word. People like him—they don't get made very often. Look at how long his career has lasted, the amount of crashes, his palmares.'

Sweet—who describes himself as a lazy cyclist who loved to race but hated to train—says that as much as they partied, Stuart always motivated him to do the hard yards. 'Especially in my last few years when I was starting to have enough of the sport. He'd say, "What do you want to do today?" and I'd say, "Go home," and he'd be like, "Come on man, I'm doing 180 km, come for a ride with me."'

According to Sweet, Stuart remained a loyal friend both on and off the bike for years even though they were on opposite teams. 'He'd ride up next to me and say, "Listen, when we turn left there's a crosswind and our team is going to put it in the gutter and try to decide the race so make sure you're at the front,"' Sweet recalls.

'We still keep in touch and when we see each other it's like it was only yesterday; we're like family and I felt so privileged to be best man at his wedding.'

There were two very different Stuarts went it came to riding and socialising. There was the Stuart everyone saw back in Australia for two months of the year—having a few beers at the local pub and enjoying myself because trying to be a normal person is a big thing to me. I sacrificed a lot during the year and loved nothing more than coming back to Adelaide and going out with mates for a long lunch in the city. Then there was the Stuart in Europe for the other ten months of the year. That Stuart doesn't even have a local pub, if you can believe it. Most Friday nights I was either in the middle of a race, travelling to a race, or preparing for a race, which meant lots of training and no time to let your hair down.

When I would finally get back to Australia at the end of the year it was time to relax. As cyclists, we get our arses kicked for 95 per cent of the year—you only win a very small percentage of races that you start—so you do a lot of losing and it can be a tough gig. Being able to release the pressure and switch off from cycling helped the longevity of my career. Whenever I started my off-season, I wouldn't want to even look at a bike for the first few weeks. There were no coffee rides with Dad, as much as he'd love to, but it just wasn't fun for me. Fun was going down the pub and having a beer with Dad, or shooting some pool or playing a game of golf.

It was not until I would wake up one morning, usually about a month after relaxing and enjoying myself back in Australia, that I would go, 'Right I want to ride *now.*' Then I flicked the switch, got back on my bike and was hungry to ride.

In my twenty years as a professional cyclist, I never let going out for a drink or having a beer at a barbecue get in the way of my training or racing. Waking up too tired or hungover was just never an option. I suppose I became hardened to it back in the early days when Henk, Jay and I would train ridiculously hard and at the end of the day fire up the barbecue. What could be more Australian than that?

In the early years of Stuart's career in Europe, he and fellow Australian Jay Sweet were virtually inseparable while training around their home in Toulouse, at barbecues and on nights out.

'I've always been a bit of a wild boy and those who know Stuey well know that he doesn't mind a drink either, so he and I just meshed straight away,' Sweet says. 'He's a redhead, he might have dyed it blonde but he's a redhead and he's fiery.'

Among memories of their escapades together is the 1998 Tour of Britain which Stuart won, with Sweet featuring on several stages. The pair went out celebrating and made it home early the next morning just in time to catch a bus to the airport.

Stuart's likeable attitude endeared him to sportspeople around the world. One of his long-time friends and personal trainers, Leigh Bryan, said this was evident during an end-of-season trip to Dublin in 2002. Celebrating the culmination of one season and planning the start of another, they ran into retired Australian football identities, including Robert DiPierdomenico, who were in town for the International Rules Series against Ireland.

'We started talking and the next thing we're going to the Aussie Gaelic footy match,' Bryan says. 'To cut a long story short, Australia won the game and we ended up on the team bus with them. So we're on the bus and the cup is being passed around full of champagne or beer and then it gets passed to Stuey. He grabbed it and skulled the whole thing and everyone on the bus just erupted. We had legend status for the rest of the night and went back to the after-party at the players' hotel.

'Everyone loves being around Stuey, he's a fun guy who always makes time for you and can develop close relationships with people from all walks of life. He's impossible not to like.'

There are plenty of urban myths about my partying and I've just about heard them all. Stories about nights out, which I haven't even had! Some guys like to exaggerate and say, 'I was out with Stuey until this hour' or 'We were at the pub and I couldn't even move and he had to race the next day.' But the best urban myth I've ever heard—and I can guarantee you it's a myth—is that I supposedly went out on the town the night before winning Paris–Roubaix in 2007. One of my young teammates, Luke Durbridge, asked me about it while we were out training one day. I said to him, 'Are you fucking joking? There is absolutely no chance in hell I'd go out the night before Paris–Roubaix ... it was two nights before.' Again, that's a joke.

The closest I came to a night out before a race was in 2004. We'd just finished the Tour de France and our next race was the Hamburg Grand Prix—or HEW Cyclassics World Cup as it was known—but in between I'd been invited to ride a criterium in Vienna. It was a one-hour race at night where we rode around like circus monkeys trying not to crash, then afterwards we were contractually obliged to go to the VIP party. So we started dropping a few big Austrian beers; one led to another and the organiser got me back to the hotel sometime after midnight.

The next morning, sitting with the boys at the airport, we were shaking our heads saying, 'What the hell?' And sure enough, the guilt kicked in and I was pissed off with myself. By the time we arrived at the hotel in Hamburg I was so tired that I went straight to bed.

The following morning at our team meeting the director

asked every guy in the room whether they wanted to win.
By now I'd had enough of always being the one who took
responsibility while others palmed the pressure on to me.
My plan was to do 150 km and re-assess at the feed zone.
Towards the end of my time at Cofidis I was putting my
hand up and riding my guts out all the time and none of
my teammates gave a shit except for one guy—Matt White.
He was the only teammate out of thirty who rode in front
of me every single race, got me drink bottles, got me food.
He was the ultimate doméstique (helper)—100 per cent
committed.

So this day in Hamburg we were cruising along in the
Cyclassics World Cup and going that slowly at the feed zone
that I couldn't bring myself to stop. We went through at 35
km/h and I looked at Whitey and said, 'What am I going to
do? I can't stop now, that's just ridiculous.' So Whitey said,
'Come on mate, you'll be right, keep going.' I got to the
final circuits of the 250 km race and thought, 'If I'm here,
I might as well have a crack.'

All of a sudden I got better and better and started attacking off the front, opened up the body and my legs came
around. Whitey brought back a big group on his own and
set it up for me. I came around the last 400 metres, did the
sprint of my life and won my first ever world cup race. It
was the biggest moment of my career at that point—bigger
than a stage win of the Tour de France. I'll cherish that
photo of me winning forever. The world champion was
second, Paolo Bettini was there, Oscar Freire, Erik Zabel,
the who's who of cycling—and little old me sticking my

hands up in the middle. It was a massive, massive win. I dedicate that victory to Matt White because without him it wouldn't have happened. Of course we went out and celebrated in style that night.

White and Stuart have known each other since 1989 when they raced the national road titles and became friends when White moved to Adelaide in 1992 on an AIS scholarship. Six months later White moved to the road program full time, but the two were reunited in the national team for the 1994 Commonwealth Games.

White says he knew of Stuart's reputation as a tough cyclist and fierce competitor, but saw it first-hand at the 1998 Commonwealth Games in Kuala Lumpur. 'Stuey was set to win the time-trial before he bit the dust and took half his freckles off. But when I saw him get up and finish the race, that's when I realised he was a real hard-arse. It was a really high-speed crash and he still finished the time-trial in second place.'

The pair roomed together at the Games and White says Stuart, never one to miss out on anything, was determined to celebrate with his teammates.

'He was in a lot of pain after the crash and the doctor came in to give him some pain killers. I started to kit up and get ready to go out for a couple of beers when I heard him say, "Whitey, can you come in here?"

'So I walk in and there he is, arm in a sling, trying to put on his shirt, telling me he's coming out with the boys. Later that night the doctor said to me, "How's Stuey going, has he gone to sleep yet?"

'"Gone to sleep?" I said. "Look at him, he's over there!" And there he was, drinking a jug of beer.'

White and Stuart grew even closer when they rode the 2000 Sydney Olympics together and then were teammates in 2004 at French team Cofidis. 'My role was working for other riders and when I got to Cofidis I started getting involved in lead-outs for Stuey,' White recalls. 'And yeah, you can work for someone, and you can work for someone—and I really did bust my balls for him because of our friendship.

'They definitely broke the mould when they made Stuey. I don't think many people realise what he's done right across the spectrum of cycling. We've had bigger road stars and bigger track stars but no one has achieved what he has across the many disciplines of cycling.'

In 2012 White took charge of Australian team Orica-GreenEDGE. That year he also directed Australia's road team at the London Olympics in which Stuart finished sixth.

'Other people have done six Olympics but no endurance athlete has done it,' White says. 'Twenty years after winning an Olympic silver medal on the track, he's in the breakaway looking like winning gold in the Olympic road race.

'It was a special moment for me to go to Stuey's last Olympics as manager because we are such good friends. And I copped a bit of criticism for even picking him in the team, people saying he was too old, but again he didn't let me down. It was one of the best results we've had in the Olympic Games men's road race.'

One night out that got plenty of media attention was during the 2010 Vuelta a España because it ended with my team boss at CSC-Saxo Bank, Bjarne Riis, throwing me and Andy Schleck off the race. Bjarne was pretty cool and he and I always had a really good relationship; in fact, he was the best manager/team director I worked under and I've got the utmost respect for him, but at times he was hard to read. One day he'd be cracking bottles of 1998 reserve chianti classico and the next day if he saw a bottle of wine he'd tell you to put it away.

Bjarne is a massive wine fanatic so we had that in common. When he came to Australia for Tour Down Under, I took him out to East End Cellars. There was a very expensive bottle of wine that Bjarne had been dreaming about drinking his whole life and he and I sat there that day and cracked it. On training camps in California he'd say, 'Okay boys, midnight curfew,' and he'd send the team home. But somehow I'd find myself still sitting at the bar with him chatting hours later.

To understand why Bjarne reacted the way he did at the

2010 Vuelta, you've got to put yourself in his shoes. At the time he had the best team in the world—Jens Voigt, the Schlecks, Fabian Cancellara, Carlos Sastre and me. Within one month we'd all jumped ship to join the Schlecks' own team at Leopard. I hadn't actually made up my mind during the Vuelta when Bjarne called me into his room and said, 'I heard you've already signed.' I said, 'Bjarne, I swear to God I haven't. Yes, the Schleckys want me to go there and yes, I'm having a talk with the owner, but I haven't signed a contract.'

Bjarne didn't believe me so it wasn't a good meeting. I walked out the door and thirty seconds later my phone rang; it was the head guy at Leopard. After the meeting with Bjarne I thought, 'You know what, I'm going,' and that's what I told Bjarne the next day even though he didn't believe that I'd only just made my decision.

At the Tour of Spain you don't usually finish dinner until 10.30 pm so Andy and I walked outside to sit in the square. It was a hot night, we'd been doing 200 km stages and we had a beer. We kicked on sitting in the square watching the world go by, then walking home we came across an Irish pub opposite our hotel. We looked at each other, looked at our watches; it was 1 am, but the stages of the Vuelta don't start until 1 pm so it wasn't like we had to be up at 7 am. I don't mind the odd Guinness so we went inside. We walked in the door and bang, who's sitting at the bar—Bjarne. He glared at us, and Andy and I must have looked like possums in the headlights as we backpedalled out of the pub and walked straight back to the hotel. In hindsight, we should have stayed and had a beer with him, but we went back to our room and listened to music. The walls were paper-thin and the team manager heard the music. The following morning Bjarne came in and said, 'You guys, this is not on, you were out all night'—which wasn't right, but I think a lot of it had to do with the tension of us leaving the team. Then he said, 'Right, you guys are off the race, pack your bags, you're going home.' And I lost it, I went off my rocker, we both said our piece and that was it. We went home.

I didn't speak to Bjarne for the rest of the year, I was that disappointed. But the following season I wrote him a letter. 'Yes, I was wrong,' I wrote, 'I shouldn't have been at a bar at 1 am, but in retrospect, how many nights have you said, "Come on Stuey, you're coming out with me tonight."'

I have absolutely no resentment towards Bjarne. I still consider him a friend and we get on fine, but it was so disappointing because the incident was taken way out of context due to us leaving the team.

Times have changed. The culture around sport is so different to what it was two decades ago; the current era is ultra-professional. Where once upon a time we wouldn't think twice about a few beers after training, now the first thing you think about is recovery, hydration, stretching, massage; and if you aren't doing that, you're falling behind everyone else. These days, going out for beers is frowned upon. There are no shenanigans during races and no messing around when you should be training. As an example of how much things have changed, on our

Orica-GreenEDGE training camp in Australia in 2012—
the first time we'd been in Australia for ten months—we
landed in Brisbane and didn't touch a drop of alcohol for
the entire ten days. It was more of a bonding than a training camp but we all decided that it wasn't a good look for
a top-level Australian team to be drinking or having any
mess-ups out on the town.

I'm not saying we're perfect. I'd like to see someone
else go to a foreign country for ten months of the year for
twenty years and live like a monk, but it's about being sen-
sible. I have certainly enjoyed myself over the years, and I
realise that's not how things are today. But I am adamant
that you can be an elite athlete and a normal bloke at the
same time. The secret is knowing when to flick the switch.

CHAPTER 9

ALL HEART

The 2002 season started with a heart problem and finished with a heart-to-heart that would dramatically alter the path of my cycling career.

The issue associated with my heart and blood-flow went undiagnosed for years, and when it was eventually discovered, it came as a shock. After the highs and lows of the 2001 Tour de France, by early 2002 I was building into another big season. I was back in Europe training and during an effort or interval my left leg would just blow up. It felt like a cramp so I'd slow down and try to shake my leg as I was riding along, guessing that it was full of lactic acid because I'd gone so hard. But it just wouldn't go away and I figured I was either over-training or not training enough.

I really started noticing it one day when I went out riding with Jay and his girlfriend. When I did an effort, I had to sit behind both of them just to get home. The pain in my leg would last a couple of hours, so I started talking about it to my team because we'd heard stories about athletes getting a blocked iliac artery. Eventually it was decided that I'd go to a local hospital for some tests. The doctors put me on a home-trainer where I had to go from stationary with no warm-up to full gas in a matter of seconds, then hold that pace until I nearly exploded. Then straight away I was thrown on a table and they took the blood pressure in both my ankles. At first they couldn't get a result on the left leg and I thought it must be the machine playing up because I was lying there sweating my arse off. So they tried again, still nothing. Eventually the doctors realised that my blood pressure was so low, there was virtually no blood getting to my left leg, with my calf muscle the worst affected.

Following the test they put me in touch with Professor Chevalier in Lyon who'd discovered this iliac artery problem in athletes. But the team had me booked in to race Het Volk and Kuurne-Brussel-Kuurne, and although I felt fine I went up to Belgium to race thinking, 'What the hell am I doing?'

I got through both races without a problem, did plenty of work and my left leg was fine. By Monday I went home scratching my head, thinking it couldn't be the iliac artery after all because I'd just ridden 400 km in two days without a glitch. But by the Wednesday I went out training and bang, the leg blew up again so this time I flew to Lyon to see the professor for more tests.

Like the other doctors, he quickly discovered there was no blood reaching my left calf. When I stopped to consider how long I'd been getting this strange feeling in my leg, I realised it had been years—so you could say that for a long time I was riding on one leg, which is kind of amazing, really.

Professor Chevalier told me the problem was reasonably common in some athletes but because they didn't know what it was, they either retired or just gave up on cycling. He realised that my career was on the line and helped me out a lot, putting me through all the tests quickly; then I went straight downstairs into an operating theatre. They injected me with dye so they could trace where the blood flowed and it showed a massive blockage in the iliac artery— a very serious problem. The iliac artery delivers blood from the abdomen to each leg, and while no one wants to hear bad news, I was relieved that they'd found it. Given that it was hindering my performance, I wanted it sorted as soon as possible. Being early February, I still had plenty of goals for later in the year so now was as good a time as any to have the operation.

I was sent some digital photos of the artery and it's hard to believe how bad it was—my artery was 10 mm wide in my left thigh and 9 mm was completely blocked. So there was a 1 mm hole where the blood could pump through. The professor said it was the worst case he'd ever seen. They don't know exactly what caused the blockage but the most likely thing was from all those years on a track bike where I was quite bent over and leaning forward.

The operation involved taking a bit of artery from my left ankle and using it to replace the blocked artery in my thigh—quite a complicated little task. It was like cutting open a hose then stitching it back up, and if there's too much pressure and you blow the hose open, you could die from internal bleeding. So the doc said in no uncertain terms that I had to go home and do absolutely nothing for a month. He said, 'If you elevate your heart-rate, you could die.'

After three frustrating weeks I finally decided to get outdoors. I've never been much of a gardener but I had to do something. Anne-Marie saw me outside mowing the lawns and told me to stop but I said, 'It's okay, I'm taking it easy.' I missed all the 2002 Classics but once I finally got back on the bike I was in a good place mentally, thinking, 'Geez, if I'd been riding on one leg all this time, imagine what I can do now that I've got two legs working properly!'

Coming back from my iliac artery operation in 2002, I realised that I had to get my shit together pretty quickly. It was mid-May and I didn't have Dad around the corner or any teammates free to motor-pace me, and Anne-Marie certainly wasn't getting on a motorbike again. But I needed someone to help me get fit really fast for the Tour de France, which I would use as preparation for the upcoming Commonwealth Games in Manchester.

So I picked up the phone and called an old mate, Leigh Bryan. Leigh was still racing as a cyclist in his own right but was coming off a big crash in America. I asked him if I could hire him as my full-time soigneur (trainer/masseur). I needed someone who was going to commit to helping me. And that's a big ask; there aren't many people in the world who'd pack up everything and help you at the drop of a hat. They might do it for a week or a month, but I needed someone full-time and I was happy to pay him to do it.

A lot of athletes try to bank every single cent they make because they think they've only got a short career and have to make every penny count. In some ways that's true, but I realised I had to invest in myself. I was getting paid a good salary and had to make the most of it; if it meant employing someone to help me, so be it.

I told Leigh—who was known to everyone as 'Rok'—that he could live with me and I'd pay him to help me train. His answer was, 'Yeah, why not,' and the next minute he was on a plane on his way to Toulouse. It was a pivotal moment in my career because his influence took me to a new level. He was making me breakfast in the mornings, giving me massages after training and I was behind that motorbike every single day. Rok turned even a coffee-shop ride into a 100 km motor-pacing session which was like race simulation and exactly what I needed to get up to speed again.

Much of the time when you're out training, you don't get much feedback. Often, your coach isn't there and there's not much he can say when you tell him how you felt on the phone afterwards. But Rok was constantly looking in the rear-vision mirrors, seeing every detail of what was going on in my body from my facial expressions. Together we made a 180 km loop around Toulouse which we called the 'form finder' because it had twenty-five climbs ranging from 1 km to 3 km long and would usually take six hours to complete. By the end of our time in Toulouse, I could do it in 4 hours 15 minutes which you'd be lucky to manage in a car.

When Rok arrived in Toulouse I told him we needed a realistic goal—to try to win the road race at the Commonwealth Games which was nine days after the end of the Tour de France. I'd never won a gold medal on the road so it was a massive incentive for me. I knew I always came out of the Tour de France in great nick and on great form, which is probably due to the thousands of kilometres of training I'd done with Charlie, so the whole time in my head during the Tour was the mantra: 'Comm Games, Comm Games.'

●

My other heart-related problem was a condition known as tachycardia which affected me as early as 1992. It was just before the semi-finals of the team pursuit at the Barcelona Olympics and we were about to go on the track so I did one more sprint on the rollers, but the next minute my heart went through the roof. Before tachycardia comes on, my heart usually skips a beat, gives a couple of big beats, then goes insane, firing away like a machine gun. The timing in Barcelona obviously wasn't ideal but I had no idea what was going on. As I got up on the track my heart-rate had been sitting on 230 bpm for five minutes, then went down to 180 but I can remember starting the team pursuit and not having any feeling in my hands or legs, and it took half a lap for it to come back.

It probably did happen at times when I was out training,

but not often enough to really worry me and evidently a lot of people have it but you might not notice it unless you're putting your body under stress.

The next time it happened during a race was on Stage 3 of the 2002 Tour de France from Metz to Reims. I was sitting in the bunch with 50 km to go and suddenly felt my heart in my chest, looked down at my heart-rate monitor and it was showing 240 bpm. I thought, 'You have got to be kidding!' so I dropped to the back of the bunch and told my team car to leave me at the back, it would go away in five to ten minutes. But unfortunately we were doing 50 km/h in a stage of the Tour de France and half an hour later it still wouldn't go down. My teammates, who were pretty concerned, dropped back and started pushing me along. All this was live on TV so there was quite a bit of attention.

Physically, what happens to me is that I find it difficult to take deep breaths; it's like my body has pins and needles. This day during the Tour I was praying to God that it would stop, but because the race was going at such high speed, I didn't have the opportunity to force my heart-rate to go down. Then, with 10 km to go, it suddenly stopped and my heart went straight back down to 140 bpm. Relieved, I decided to still go for the sprint and, despite my team telling me to take it easy, I managed to finish tenth even though I hadn't gone all-in.

The following day was a rest day and the organisers of the Tour de France made me go to hospital for some tests. The doctors told me they were going to bring on an episode of tachycardia that would tell them if it was that career-threatening. I was pretty nervous—more so because to bring on tachycardia they actually make your heart stop for a couple of seconds which feels like an eternity—then it kicks back in. I had to hang around for the results and, anxious that they could potentially end my career, it was an uncomfortable wait. But the doctors came back and said, 'It's not career-threatening, you can continue,' so I walked out and went back to the hotel thinking, 'Beauty, the show would go on.' Ever since then, it has happened less and less, and while I might notice it every now and then sitting on the couch, it's never bothered me.

With the tachycardia drama of the Tour de France behind me, it was on to Manchester for the Commonwealth Games. We took an awesome team, including Cadel Evans who was becoming a big hitter in world cycling, and Cookey (Baden Cooke) who was closing in on winning a green jersey, so every country was expecting us to win. At the team meeting we decided we were all capable of winning the 187 km race; it was just a matter of who and how we'd do it.

On race day, we got straight on the front and let a group go. On the sixteen-lap course there were two major climbs, the second of which everyone expected us to attack over the top. But just before we hit the first climb, the peloton had to thin out because we went over a small bridge; it was like sand going through an hourglass.

After we'd done a few laps I said to the boys, 'How about we go full gas into this bridge; we'll be on the front when guys are still hitting the brakes and we'll attack up the first climb.' It was one of those rare races where the script in your head actually works out perfectly. Sure enough, I ended up getting away from the bunch on the first climb, Cookey and Cadel covered any move that would come from the peloton, and I rode solo to the finish line for a Commonwealth Games gold medal on the road. It was a really special moment, particularly given what had happened in the few months before, but also knowing the calibre of the guys in our team and that anyone could have won. In the end, Cadel attacked and finished second, and Cookey wrapped up what was left of the peloton to grab third spot so we were all on the podium, which was pretty cool for Australia.

It was a very satisfying way to end the season after all the drama of my iliac artery operation, month off the bike, then tachycardia at the Tour de France.

After Manchester, Rok and I and another mutual friend went to Dublin to toast a successful comeback from my health scares and to plan the new season ahead. As it turned out, that trip would prove crucial to the next few years of my career.

Leigh Bryan recalls the defining moment of their trip to Dublin when he and Stuart had a heart-to-heart conversation.

'I told Stuey that I believed he should adjust his focus from the

Tour de France and to target the spring Classics. I believed this was where he could really excel and it would not be detrimental to his Tour form, but it was going to require a huge amount of planning and a massive commitment from both of us if we were to do it properly,' Bryan says.

'He was going to need to have trust and faith in the daily process I would implement as now all forms of training and recovery were to become his priority. We needed to be more selective about what type of workload he did, both on and off the bike, to ensure he made use of his best physical condition and form at the right times during the season. The natural talent he'd been relying on was still there but now he needed to work with more structure and intelligence to attain his objectives.'

In the months leading up to that trip to Dublin, I'd realised that Rok was a key element to my success in Manchester because the work we did paid dividends straight away. When we first started working together, I was the one telling him what I needed to do; but Rok has a strong background in physical education, he is a bike-rider and a smart guy who knows a lot about physiology and the human mind. He was also very good at telling me the truth, he wasn't afraid to call it as it he saw it or to put his ideas forward. It was really important for me to have someone to bounce ideas off because life in Toulouse was pretty solitary at times. I didn't have another coach to talk to, or anyone besides Anne-Marie to confide in, and I didn't like bringing my work home. I wouldn't sit around the dinner table and tell Anne-Marie, 'I just did five hours and all these efforts.' Rok, however, would fit right in to that conversation. We'd been friends for a long time so it was the perfect relationship because he was also a mentor for me.

Before any big occasion—Olympic Games, Paris–Roubaix—I'd always phone him just before the race to tell him how I saw the event unfolding, as though it was a film in my head. 'Every dog has his day mate, what do you reckon?' I'd say. Because ultimately, no matter how much training you've done, one of the most important ingredients for any bike-rider is confidence.

After my conversation with Rok in Dublin, I decided to go for the Classics. I was done chasing the green jersey at the Tour de France, I'd been up there but if it was going to happen it would have happened by now, so we shifted our focus to races like Paris–Roubaix and Tour of Flanders. I thought I was more suited to Flanders because Roubaix guys tend to be bigger with legs twice the size of mine so they could handle the cobbles better. Flanders was a race I thought I could maybe win; it was one of those out-there dreams. Flanders has more climbs so there's a thinner field when the race gets interesting at the end and, unlike Paris–Roubaix where guys can sprint into each sector and come in kamikaze-style, Flanders is hard, twisty and windy with 20 per cent (gradient) climbs so the field thins out selectively.

Milan–San Remo was another spring Classic I wanted to believe I could win, but I knew there was always going to be someone quicker than me in the final. I had some success in that race—third in 2004, fourth in 2005 and fifth in 2007—but never quite the ultimate success. I wasn't a pure sprinter like Alessandro Petacchi or Erik Zabel; they were quicker than me and there was nothing I could do about it.

My new training regime with Rok started in Australia in December 2002. He had me in the gym—something I'd never done in my life—but now I was there four or five times a week. I used to do my strength training on the road by riding up and down a hill in a massive gear. But Rok was using the gym to get my head away from the bike.

The strength came quite quickly, so one day I said to him that I really wanted to win a national championship before I retired so I could wear the Australian jersey in Europe and at the Tour de France. This then became our first target and we trained bloody hard. We went to the Bay Criterium Series in Melbourne and every morning I'd do two to three hours before the criterium, ride to the event, do the race and ride home—so I was clocking up 180–200 km a day with an hour of racing in the middle; I knew that no other bike-rider was doing that. On one occasion we rode back to Geelong from Ocean Grove and racked up 280 km because I was that focused on winning the national championship. By the time we got to Ballarat in January for the 2003 national championships I knew my form was good and I'd done everything possible to put myself in a winning position.

The course was around Buninyong in Victoria. I got in the early move because I didn't want to have to chase everything later on. I made the race very hard then attacked up every climb until it was down to me, Allan Davis and Patty Jonker. I managed to beat them to win my first national title.

Patty's a good mate but he's never been the quickest guy in a sprint. Davis, on the other hand, was one of the most talented young sprinters coming through the ranks so I knew I had a race on my hands. But everything just worked out for me and when I crossed the finish line it was a mix of emotions—joy and relief but ultimately satisfaction that Rok and I had targeted a race, trained hard and I'd been able to deliver. It marked the start of something special.

CHAPTER 10

CLOSE TO HOME

I've made so many friends in cycling over the journey. We've laughed and celebrated the highs, and comforted each other and cried at the lows. I know I'm biased but I doubt there's a closer bond between a sporting team than what exists in professional road cycling. We are on the road with each other for hundreds of days each year; we room together, eat together, relax together and ride, hurt and fight like hell during a race together. Everything we achieve is a result of the sacrifice and dedication of our teammates. Without them we are nothing. But it's not unusual for a cyclist to have at least three different teams throughout his career so sometimes, just as you've built that bond with your teammates, it's time to move on and start again. But a bond with your best mates is unbreakable, whether you're riding together or not. And so it was with Scottish cyclist Dave Millar.

Dave and I met while we were both living in Toulouse in the late 1990s. Our careers were just starting out but the main reason we became friends was because we were among a select few English-speaking riders in the peloton.

Although we had much in common, Dave and I had come to cycling from very different paths. I had come through an institution, the AIS, where we had our own mechanic, coach, masseur and anything we needed. Dave, on the other hand, had to make his own way a lot of the time and did it a lot tougher. In Europe in those days if you weren't French, Italian or Spanish it was very hard to break into the professional cycling scene. There were horror stories of guys going up to Belgium and living on one baguette a day because they struggled to make enough money to feed themselves. That's where we differed from the Europeans—we wanted it so bad. Cycling wasn't just a hobby or a pastime to guys who came from Australia or the UK; it was everything, and if we didn't give 100 per cent, we were finished. So Dave and I could really relate to each other, but because of my long-term relationship with Roger Legeay, it wasn't until 2004 that we finally became teammates.

As I gradually began to expect, the 2003 season proved to be my last with Roger at Crédit Agricole. I took my winning form from the national titles to record my best result to date in a Classic with third place in the Tour of Flanders.

It was a typical Tour of Flanders—hard and fast and one of the toughest I can remember because of the climbs and speed of the race. There were a flurry of attacks in the last few kilometres and because I was the only rider left from my team in the last 50 or 60 km, I had to be really careful with my moves and where I used my energy. I went on the attack a couple of times and about eight of us got away with all the big hitters. We came into one of the hardest climbs, the Muur, when Peter Van Petegem and Frank Vandenbroucke attacked and left us in their dust. After that we were racing for third place and I managed to wrap up the sprint to land a spot on the podium alongside the two Belgian stars.

From that day I realised I was capable of winning a Classic because I'd achieved it with minimal help from my team. The Classics quickly became the new number one objective in my cycling life, but to win one I realised that I needed to be in a team where I had much more support in the final. So I came away from that Classics campaign doing a lot of hard thinking. During the Tour de France, Thor Hushovd had really started coming along and I could sense my time at Crédit Agricole was probably up. It all came to a head in the Tour that year when Thor and I were teammates but basically sprinting against each other, me down the left side of the road and Thor on the right.

The 2003 Tour wasn't a disaster for me, far from it. I managed to win the Centenary Classification of that year's race which was quite special. It was decided by awarding points to the best-placed riders in the six stage finishes that matched stages from the 1903 edition of the race—in Lyon, Marseille, Toulouse, Bordeaux, Nantes and Paris. It worked like golf where the lowest score wins; so if you were first into a stage you got one point, second got two points and so on.

Coming into the final time-trial on the penultimate stage in Nantes, Thor and I were sitting first and second in the classification. I hadn't been keeping an eye on it but at dinner the night before the stage, we realised that whoever was fastest in the 49 km individual time-trial the following day would win the special Centenary Classification, which meant going up on the podium in Paris, a trophy and 100,000 Euros. So it was game on.

The following day I went out and unleashed one of the best time-trials I'd done in years, finishing eleventh, 1 minute 38 seconds down on Dave Millar's winning time. But more importantly, I was ahead of Thor who also went pretty well but was 27th, a further 51 seconds back. So in the end, I won the classification and the prize-money, which was split among the team.

At the post-Tour party in Paris I was still getting the vibe from Roger that after nine years it was time for me to leave. When it finally happened, the first person I called was Dave because he had a lot of influence in selecting riders for his own team at Cofidis. He gave the boss a ring and because I'd just finished third in the Tour of Flanders and Cofidis had a strong Classics team but didn't have a leader, there was a position for me. Within 24 hours of calling Dave, I received a fax with a contract offer and it was all signed a couple of weeks after the Tour de France. I would be riding officially for French team Cofidis in 2004.

Dave and I had been mates for a long time but for him to go out of his way to get me on the team showed his commitment to our friendship. We then became roommates, I'd travel to Biarritz in our downtime for a swim at the beach, and he'd do the same by coming to Toulouse to hang out every now and then.

I was genuinely excited by the opportunities that lay ahead when I joined Dave at Cofidis in January 2004, even though it was the first time I would miss my home race, the Tour Down Under, because of a training camp in Spain. Unfortunately, my excitement didn't last long. Flying back into Paris after the camp I had a connecting flight to Toulouse. As we were wandering through Charles de Gaulle airport, there were suddenly police everywhere. They were going after some of my teammates and it was a pretty strange period. I didn't see anyone getting handcuffed but I heard about it when I got to my departure gate.

Still in shock and not knowing what had happened, I called Dave while I waited for my flight to Toulouse, but he didn't answer. The next minute on the news, bang: 'Cofidis scandal' and 'doping ring' headlines were flashing across the TV screen. It was a really uncomfortable moment. I'd come into a brand new team, I didn't know three-quarters of the riders and staff, and suddenly we were surrounded by controversy.

When I got home I watched it all unfold on television, trying to understand as best I could with my limited French. I had a lot of questions and I wanted answers but the information coming through was pretty vague because the police were involved. We had a team meeting soon after and we voted to bring in internal team drug-testing. We continued racing for the early part of the Classics season and I went to Milan–San Remo with great form. It was the first time I got to captain this new outfit and the whole team was there to ride for me. I finished third behind Oscar Freire and Erik Zabel and was really happy with my performance because I had delivered on my first big race for my new team.

But a few weeks later in April, the team decided to suspend all racing pending the ongoing doping investigation at our team. It made me really bitter because I knew I was in great shape and was just so desperate to race, but for the first time I had to sit at home and watch Paris–Roubiax unfold without me.

It was a really low time for me; I'd done everything I could to be in good form but when something happens that's completely out of your control, you feel helpless and I was devastated.

I'd met a heap of Australian rugby players in Toulouse so I invited them around for a barbecue to watch Paris–Roubaix. I tried to make a day of it, but to be honest it sucked because I was meant to be racing. The only good thing about watching the race was seeing my good mate and former teammate Magnus Backstedt win.

I soon realised that I could look at the situation two ways. The easy option was to say, 'Stuff it, the team has been suspended,' and just throw in the towel. But at the same time I understood the steps the team needed to take to protect itself and come out of this with a better image. My other option was to train like a man possessed.

No matter what happened at Cofidis, I still had the Athens Olympics coming up, which was really important to me. So instead of throwing in the towel, I used my bike to unleash my fury on the roads while out training. I'd be out riding in Cofidis clothing and people would yell abuse at me, things like 'doper', which really fired me up. Yes, I'd made a mistake in the past but this abuse was unjustified. I had moved on, re-focused and didn't want to be cast in that mould for the rest of my life. If you stole something when you're a teenager does that mean you are a thief for the rest of your life?

So I trained my arse off and every single ride was behind Rok on the motorbike; we clocked up some serious kilometres. I have always said that when something happens in life, quite often you're not going to understand the reason, there's no logic to it, but you've got to deal with it. My way of dealing with it was to be out doing 150 km behind the motorbike. As I rode, I would say to myself, 'I'm going to prove to you bastards what we're capable of.'

The team was eventually back racing in time for the Criterium du Dauphine in June 2004. I stepped straight in and won stages 5 and 7; then my heart was set on winning the points classification.

Going into the final stage I had the green jersey and we faced a 200 km mountain stage into Grenoble. I was pretty pissed off about this because it meant a sprinter was unlikely to win the green jersey. So we went out on an absolute mission. Dave and I went out in a break and I got through the mountains but was dropped on the last climb. But I really dug deep and caught the French rider at the top, then I did the descent from hell—it was one of the fastest, maddest descents I've ever done. This time I had both wheels skipping off the road around each corner, I was pushing everything to the absolute limit and was in the zone. Fear was never in my mind, only complete concentration. I was braking with everything I had on the front wheel and steadily pumping the back brake. This is something a lot of riders don't know how to do properly—if you brake too much on the back, you risk locking up the rear wheel which means you go straight ahead, ultimately leading to a crash. It's an art form bombing down a mountain at warp speed, adrenaline pumping, using every centimetre of the road, constantly watching for changing tarmac, gravel and wet spots all while being kept upright by 3 mm of rubber. When you're doing it right, it's so much fun; you're at one with your machine and it's the best feeling you can have on a bike.

On that day I rode solo to victory to win the stage and green jersey, so mission accomplished. My form was right on target and everything was good again.

But then it all changed. Again.

I was at home in Toulouse on 23 June 2004 when I got a call from a friend saying Dave had been arrested while at a restaurant in Biarritz. Police could have done it nice and quietly but they decided to make it a big, public Hollywood scene and arrest him in front of everyone. I was shocked, it was another blow and probably the biggest blow of all because it was a mate—I didn't want to believe it.

One of the first questions I asked Dave when I called him was, 'Is this true, did you actually do it?' When he did confess, he got out of France for a while. I was really worried about his health and just wanted him to know that while it seemed that everyone had dropped him like a hot potato, his true friends would always be there for him. I told him that whatever had happened couldn't be changed, but he still had a life to consider and a future and I wanted him to know he had some support.

Dave came to Toulouse after a while and we hung out. He was in the darkest of dark holes and I wanted to be there for him. I wanted to listen to his story, and he was very open and honest about it all. He was thrown in jail and treated like an axe murderer and I couldn't see how that punishment fit the crime. Maybe that's because I'd made a mistake too and gotten away with it, but I was never tempted to tell him what I'd done. It was something I wanted to take to my grave; I was so ashamed of it that I didn't ever want to open up about it to anyone.

Millar says he and Stuart were trying to survive in a world that wasn't nice and was 'the dark ages of cycling'.

'I had no idea we had actually done the same thing—dope, that is. When I was doping I never told Stuey about it; similarly, he never told me what he'd done. I'm guessing he had come to his conclusions with regards to what I was up to, and by that time he had chosen a different path.

'I can now understand part of the reason why he was so understanding towards me when he saw my life fall apart in 2004 after my arrest and doping confession. It's strange how we could be so close and yet still ashamed to share that, the most important of things, but that's how dark the world was and how much we disliked ourselves for having crossed a line we never were meant to.

'I now know why he never judged me. He helped me out a lot and was always there for me through my ban to this day, and no doubt he'll be there for the rest of our lives. I hope I can be as good a friend to him as he has been to me.'

As shocking as it was, and on top of everything that had already happened to our team that year, I still didn't want to hang up my bike. Blow after blow kept coming but I saw each one as a new challenge. I was super-determined that year, but I was also angry. Why was this happening to me? Why this team? You could search for answers as long as you like but I found the best answer on the bike. I went to the Tour de France that year knowing I had trained hard, and aiming for a stage win.

From the start I was up against it after losing my most

loyal teammate in Matt White, whose first Tour de France was over before it even began. On the morning of the prologue in Liège we left the team bus to do a lap of the course and there were people everywhere. As we were riding along I noticed a little speed-hump up ahead hiding all the TV camera cables. Just as I turned around to tell Whitey to watch out, doing 10 km an hour, he t-boned it and went straight over the handlebars, snapping his collarbone.

Stage 5 on 8 July was a hard, wet, cold, rainy, crap day and we had to ride 200 km from Amiens to Chartres. I had to use a lot of experience in the final, I attacked and went solo, thought I had it in the bag but they caught me so I had to re-shuffle my tactics. Then I attacked again, put my head down and sprinted like crazy. I ended up winning in a small sprint that gave me the green jersey before Robbie McEwen took it all the way to Paris.

The stage win was a huge moment for me and the team. We'd come back from an absolute disaster at the start of the year and by July we were having a champagne shower. I shaved the team director, Francis van Londersele's head as promised if I won a stage of the Tour. But the win had extra special meaning for me because I dedicated it to Dave. I wanted him to know that he was the reason I was on that team and that life is a rollercoaster. You can go from the lowest of lows to the highest of highs in weeks or months and what doesn't kill you makes you stronger. There was a lot of emotion in that victory salute as I crossed the line, a big double-arm punch in the air. I spoke about Dave in my media interviews. People make mistakes and people pay for it and I wanted him to get his life back on track.

I always finished the Tour de France in good nick so after a few recovery days I was back behind the motorbike doing some crazy training. The world cup win in Hamburg was the biggest of my career to that point. As mentioned earlier, I went to that race thinking I'd just take it easy but when I got there and Whitey worked so hard to bring the race back together, I found myself with a perfect opportunity to sprint for the win. Winning was massive and all of a sudden I was being talked about as one of the favourites for the upcoming Olympic road race. I had Olympic gold on my mind alright—just not in the race that everyone expected.

Earlier that year, Bryan had realised that with a full week between the road race and madison at the Athens Olympics, Stuart was a chance to do both events.

'We hadn't spoken about it, but we stopped for a coffee out training and I just threw it at him, "What do you think about riding the madison at the Olympics? It's eight days after the road race so you can come home to Toulouse, rest, recover, do some good training then head back to Athens. Why don't you call Shayne Bannan and have a chat about it?"

'Stuey can tend to procrastinate to avoid confrontation sometimes so when he said "Yeah, I'll call him later" I didn't want to give him an option so I simply grabbed his phone off the table and said, "You need to make that call right now and we are not leaving here until you do."'

When Rok suggested I take part in the madison, I just laughed at him and thought, 'Whatever, I'm not doing the track, it's not possible. Surely you've got to qualify and there would be a rule making it impossible for me to race.' But he had planted a seed in the back of my mind. He told me to ring Shayne and wouldn't take no for an answer. So I mustered up the courage and said, 'G'day Shayne, it's Stuey here ... Now I know this is pretty left-field, but what are the chances of me riding the madison at the Olympics?' Shayne paused and said, 'I wasn't expecting that call, but leave it with me and I'll get in touch with Ian McKenzie.'

Ian was the head of the track endurance team. In the next day or two Shayne rang back and said it looked like it could be possible. Because I was on the road team, it qualified me for any cycling event at the Olympics, so I wouldn't have to race a track event leading in. Rok had two conditions on me doing the madison as well as the road race: it was to remain a secret for as long as possible to avoid unnecessary scrutiny and pressure, and that I be allowed to return to Toulouse after the road race so I could train properly and prepare. I also wanted it kept quiet, mainly because I wanted to make sure it was happening, but also I didn't want to piss off another rider who'd been training his arse off for the last four or eight years only for some professional road rider to stick his hand up and say, 'I'll do that.'

It was a big shot in the dark for Ian McKenzie. I hadn't been on a track bike for four years so it was a massive risk for him; to this day I still thank him for giving me that opportunity. Look at it from his perspective: he gets a random phone call from a road racer wanting to just 'pop in' for the Olympics. Who in their right mind would say, 'Yeah, no problem,' unless they knew I could do the job. But I'd proven myself on the road, there was no question my form was going to be good. It was just a matter of making the Australian selectors believe it could be possible.

According to McKenzie, despite Stuart's four-year absence from the track, his decision to nominate for the Athens Olympics did not come as a shock. 'I wasn't particularly surprised because I knew he was desperate for an Olympic gold medal, he had this burning desire. To be honest, I was actually quite pleased when I got the call from Shayne,' McKenzie says.

'The selectors and I didn't believe we had a strong enough team to win medals. It was a bit of a roll of the dice and it was my decision, but I gambled on Stuart because I knew he would be in super form, that year he was probably at his peak. I'd seen him previously off no track preparation step straight into national level racing and perform.'

After making the call to Shayne, I remember putting the phone down on the table and saying to Rok, 'Can you imagine in a few months if we're sitting around with a gold medal? How funny would that be?'

CHAPTER 11

WORTH THE WAIT IN GOLD

Once I got the all-clear to ride the track at the 2004 Olympics, I suddenly got very nervous. You don't forget how to ride on a velodrome but I hadn't been in that environment for a long time; in fact, the last time I had ridden a madison was at the Adelaide SuperDrome in the 1990s. Brett Aitken and I were a pretty deadly madison combination in the early days; we won the national championship a couple of times and also the Bendigo Madison, which is one of the most famous races in Australia at over 100 km on an outdoor velodrome.

With my sudden inclusion in the team, it obviously meant someone had to make way. I was told that Mark Renshaw probably would have ridden the madison if I didn't. Displacing another rider was one of the reasons I was hesitant about the whole thing initially. I knew what it was like to be part of an Australian team pursuit and the years of work that go into it. You're basically training for four years on hardly any money, all of it geared towards one race that lasts for four minutes.

Thankfully, it has never been awkward with me and Mark. At the end of the day, we were both candidates for one position and it was up to selectors, who I guess realised that I had the Tour de France in my legs and I'd had success in the past, so it was a gamble worth taking.

By early 2004, still only a handful of people knew what was going on—Rok, Ian McKenzie, Shayne Bannan and Anne-Marie. The bloke I was going to ride with, Graeme Brown, didn't even know until he was called in to a meeting with Shayne and Ian a few weeks before the Games; that's how secretive it was.

When I look back on it now, it was pretty amazing. I was a professional road cyclist so even though I was doing the madison, my number one objective was still the 224 km Olympic road race. If I could tailor-make a course to suit me, the Athens race wasn't it, but when I'd checked it out the year before, I realised how hard it was, which would work to my advantage. Throw in the heat, and it was like riding in a pizza oven so I knew it would take a tough bike-rider to win the gold medal.

The road race went fairly smoothly and we did everything we could, but in the end Italian Paolo Bettini attacked where we all knew he would and rode to the gold medal while the rest of us were left to scramble around for the minor medals. Sergio Paulinho and Axel Merckx attacked in the final to win silver and bronze. I led Robbie McEwen out in the sprint and he finished eleventh while I was back in 33rd place, so a solid race but nothing special.

The team went out for a few beers that night and we talked about the race, then the following morning I flew back to Toulouse so I could spend the week recovering and training for the madison. It was impossible to train in Athens. Being in the athletes' village can be very distracting because it's such an exciting place; you can sit in the food hall people-watching for hours and suddenly half the day is gone. I knew this would probably be my last Olympics—or my last realistic shot at Olympic gold at least—so I did not want to stuff anything up.

When I got home I had two rest days then was back behind the motorbike for 150 km and doing race simulation, which is about preparing the body for what it's about to do. I knew that no one else in the madison field would be doing that because at the velodrome in Athens, you'd have a half-hour time slot to ride, if you were lucky.

Despite my nerves, the week went really quickly. I flew back to Athens two days before the race with Anne-Marie and Seth because I had a feeling that something good was going to happen and I wanted them to witness it. It was a pretty gutsy thing to do because it was 10 pm when we arrived and Seth was only eighteen months old. I put him and Anne-Marie in a taxi to a hotel while I headed to the athletes' village. By this stage it was 11 pm and I was on a bus with no idea where I was going. I didn't know where the Australian quarters were or even which room I was staying in.

But just as the bus pulled up at the village, a guy got off in front of me: it was long-time Australian swimming coach Laurie Lawrence whom I'd met a few times at previous Olympics. It was a massive blessing to find someone who knew what was going on.

I finally got to my room at 11.30 pm where my roommate, track sprinter Ryan Bayley, was fast asleep. Everything in the village was quiet.

Waking up the next morning surrounded by all the track guys was like a trip back in time; I felt totally out of place. I'd been out of the system for so long, hadn't been to any camps or world championships. But all the riders were really cool and a couple of them lightened the mood by telling me, 'Don't forget you always turn left on the velodrome, Stuey.'

The entire Australian track cycling team was on a mission that week and the gold medals started to flow. One night Ryan came back to our room with a gold medal and just flung it on the bed; it struck me that I was rooming with the Olympic sprint champion! I looked at his medal and the pressure valve went up.

Then he walked in with another gold medal, this time for the keirin—again, flinging it on the bed as if to say, 'How do you like them apples?'

He wasn't the only person getting medals. The team pursuit boys absolutely blitzed their event so another four gold medals came banging down the hallway. With each gold medal that came swinging past me I thought, 'Holy shit, I've really got to do something here.' Browny, my madison partner, was a member of the team pursuit quartet that won gold and I became like his dad saying, 'Don't you go out too late celebrating tonight, get your arse to bed.' It was hard for him because all the other boys had finished their racing, but to Browny's credit he kept the celebrations to a minimum until our madison was over.

Outside of the Australian team, no one knew about my upcoming madison event until one morning I went for a ride with Browny. As we headed back to the food hall I noticed all the cyclists' bikes were parked out the front. I walked in and British riders Bradley Wiggins and Rob Hayles looked at me and said, 'Oh, you've decided to hang around for a while and party?' And I said, 'Na, I'm doing the madison.' I can't remember what they said but their reaction was a cross between a nervous laugh and a 'you're kidding me' look.

It was the same when I eventually got to the velodrome for training and saw Matt Gilmore, an old teammate of mine who was now racing for Belgium. Besides Wiggo and Hayles, they were the hot favourites for the event. I looked down behind the motorbike and saw Matt walk into the velodrome. When he noticed me, the expression on his face was: 'What the hell are you doing here?'

I did a few practice hand-changes with Browny because it's extremely important to get that aspect right in a madison. It may look easy on TV or from the grandstand but you make one mistake throwing your teammate into the race at 60 km/h and not only are you going to rip one of your arms off but there's a very good chance of a crash which would wreck everything. It's hard enough doing it when there are just two of you on the track let alone throwing in twenty other teams which is absolute mayhem.

Brown says he had no problems staying motivated for the madison after winning team pursuit gold. His only concern was being able to keep up with Stuart when they started racing.

'I walked in with my gold medal and he had this concerned look on his face as if he thought I didn't care about the madison anymore but I said, "Don't worry Stuey, I'm greedy."

McKenzie's enduring memory of Stuart's Athens campaign was the look on the faces of opposition riders when they saw him enter the velodrome. 'They were shitting themselves. Stuart had just won the Hamburg World Cup and it was like [Eddy] Merckx walking in.'

Boarding the bus on race day I was nervous as hell worrying if I had everything in my bag; I was like a little kid going to school. Sitting at the front of the bus was Ian McKenzie. I felt that I had to thank him, so I walked up and said, 'Ian, I just want to say again that whatever happens, thanks very much for giving me the opportunity to be here.' Ian just looked at me and without even a flinch or a moment's hesitation said, 'You're not going to let me down, are you Stuey?' I curled up in my tracksuit and said, 'No, no mate, of course not,' and walked to the back of the bus thinking, 'What the hell have I got myself in for?'

Entering the velodrome was like walking into the Colosseum with people in the stands and gladiators waiting to do battle. I put on my shoes and looked around thinking, 'Here I am, hey, the Olympics on the track, so much has happened in between but I'm back to my roots again.'

Because it had been such a covert operation, Browny and I didn't have months beforehand to discuss tactics so I just said, 'Look mate, we've obviously never ridden a madison together but I can see you're on pretty good form. I haven't ridden one for a long time but every one that I have won, we were aggressive and I've attacked.' I knew I had form and hundreds of thousands of kilometres in my legs so strength wouldn't be a problem but I was pretty worried about the speed of the race. In my limited knowledge of watching the other teams, I knew the Spaniards waited until the end to take a lap on the field because they didn't have the speed to take the points. So I told Browny, 'Follow for the first couple, try and grab some points but don't try to win the first sprint. Then bang, when everyone does the third sprint, we hit it full tilt and try to get a lap and basically just bloody hang on from there.' I was trying to get in his head that we needed to be aggressive; we could not afford to hang back. It was only a 50 km race so I wasn't worried about the distance, we just had to give it a red-hot crack.

It wasn't until I got to the start line that I realised I'd forgotten a lot of the rules of madison racing. I forgot what happened if I punctured or crashed. One rider starts and the other guy lines up on the other side of the track and Browny and I hadn't even spoken about any of this stuff so I said, 'You start mate because I've got no idea what's going on here, I'm just going to follow one of the other riders who has plenty of experience.' All the nerves were getting to boiling point and I just wanted to get this race started because the build-up had been so intense. Once I'd got going, I knew I'd go into autopilot and everything else would become a kaleidoscope of colour and noise around me. I wanted to be in the zone.

It didn't take long because we started really well, got the first few changes out of the way quickly, which was a big relief, and were soon flying along at 60 km/h and attacked. We got the lap and so did Germany but I knew that we were on.

In a madison you've only got a second or two to speak to the other rider as you're grabbing his hand and I remember yelling at Browny, 'Let's go!' I wanted him to attack first because he had the sprint and raw power to get a gap, then he'd throw me in and I'd have the strength to turn that into a lap on the field. After 138 laps of the 200-lap race, Browny had a go and we were quickly shut down but as soon as he threw me in, I had this killer instinct.

Now it was a matter of making sure we kept getting points but I didn't want to rest on what I thought would be enough; I wanted to keep driving the nail in the coffin, there was no way I was slowing down. I won the very next sprint which put us into the lead on eight points with Germany second on five. I was thinking, 'There's less than 25 km to go, that's nothing.' I guess that's where the road mentality takes over. I wanted to be consistent with the sprints and we were. We took points on every sprint and took the lead in the race as I kept throwing Browny in saying, 'Come on mate, this is for the gold!' He was trying to tell me to relax but I wasn't listening; it was one of those rides that no matter how hard I went, I didn't feel a thing and don't remember suffering.

As the race wore on I was on that much of a buzz and adrenaline rush that I was having the time of my life. The stars had finally aligned and this was my time to get the gold medal. My only worry was being really thirsty because the crazy thing about this race is you can't have any outside assistance, you can't even get a drink—which is pretty medieval given you're riding 55 km/h for 50 km. I was so thirsty I was trying to find moisture on my skinsuit but even the sweat had dried up. My mouth was the sorest part of my whole body, which was cooking.

The Spanish started their attacks pretty late in the race, as I expected, and we shut every one of them down. I was having that good a day that they attacked with everything they had and a couple of times got quite big gaps but I just shut them down. That's when you know you're on fire on the track—when you can go 'bang' and kill any gap, then as soon as they'd swing up I'd attack them because I wasn't finished, I wanted to hurt them in return.

Even when Browny won the second-last sprint to secure us the gold medal I didn't have time to become emotional because the race was still going. Coming into the last sprint I knew we were about to win gold but I was still yelling to Browny, 'This is it, another gold for you, come on mate!' I lined up and knew I didn't have to win it but I didn't want to lose it either.

When I crossed the line it was a dream come true. Even though we'd won, there's a photo of me looking quite angry. Of course I wasn't angry but it was sixteen years of pressure, of built-up frustration, finally coming out all at once. Suddenly thoughts were going through my head at a million miles an hour; I had flashbacks of my first bike, of joining SASI, going to Barcelona, Atlanta, Sydney and missing out, of riding hundreds of thousands of kilometres, sometimes in the rain and hurting like you wouldn't believe. Now finally it was absolute, pure relief, which a few seconds later turned to joy. Browny and I had won by 22 points and a lap on the field while Switzerland and Great Britain were next on 10 points.

As I started slowing down it hit me, it's almost indescribable, like I was on another planet. The first thing I did was find Browny, then got over to the side of the track to find my family. Anne-Marie and Seth were there to greet me and if I wasn't crying then I wasn't far from it. I threw my helmet and glasses into the crowd and it's lucky the bike didn't go over as well.

'I remember lying on the floor in the pits calling my missus to say we'd won but that was all I had. I could not have done another lap. Stuey was ridiculous; I don't think I could have won with any other partner,' Brown says.

That night we caught up with our families then took our gold medal—our VIP entry into any club we wanted—into town. When I eventually got back to the village in the early hours of the next morning, I walked into my room and just like Ryan had done twice, finally got to throw my own gold medal on the bed.

Brown says he knew he was in for a big night out when he and Stuart were on the bus on the way in to the city to celebrate. 'We got back to the athletes' village, had some McDonald's and went for a shower. I was so tired I just wanted to go to bed. By then it was already after midnight but I heard a knock on the door and someone saying, "Browny, you ready?"

'We were on our way into town and Stuey said, "Shit Browny, I've got to go to the bank, I've only got 500 Euros." I remember thinking, "What are we in for here?"

'I only had two drinks that night, I just couldn't do it. I left and the next time I saw Stuey was in the morning.'

While winning Olympic gold with Stuart is one of the most memorable moments of Brown's career, he remembers what unfolded weeks later just as clearly.

'At the time Australia Post paid athletes $18,000 for every gold medal they won at the Olympics. In our case it was to be split $9000 each,' Brown says.

'The night of our win we were high-fiving each other and I said, "That's half my yearly salary." Stuey turned to me and said, "Well, you can have my share mate."

'I told him he didn't have to do that. In all the emotion of the moment, it's very easy to say things like that. A few days later I told Dad about it and he said, "Well, just wait and see."

'Then about a month later I got a call from Stuey saying, "Browny, what are your bank details? That money has come through."

There's no doubt my career would have felt a bit empty without winning that gold medal. To me, the Olympics has always been the epitome of sport. No Tour de France or world championship or Classic can replace an Olympic gold medal; I guess that's the Australian in me. We take the Olympics very seriously and have a great history of Olympic legends. Coming through school and starting cycling, all I wanted to do was represent Australia at the Olympics. At Barcelona we came so close to gold and I thought my chance had gone up in smoke, so to finally get it twelve years later was massive.

Anne-Marie says she'd never seen her husband so happy as in the moments immediately after the race. 'That was the first time I had seen him race on the track because I'd missed all his track years. To see him win gold was by far one of the most exciting moments of our lives.'

After the Olympics I still had good form and it would have been a shame to waste it so I went back to my road team for the rest of the season, which was proving to be my vintage year. Podium in Milan–San Remo, winning stages in the Dauphine, the Tour de France, the Hamburg World Cup, the Olympics—it just kept rolling along so I went back to the pro peloton with a different kind of confidence. All of a sudden I wasn't only Stuart O'Grady the stage winner of the Tour and wearer of the yellow jersey, I was Olympic champion and with that came another level of respect. I went to the Vuelta a España and did some great sprints with eight top-ten finishes, had the points jersey and was second on one of the most difficult stage finishes I'd ever done in my life.

It was Stage 10, 174 km from Alcoi to Xorret de Cati, which finished with a Category 1 climb, and I was in a breakaway with Erik Zabel and Oscar Freire. As a sprinter I wasn't expected to be anywhere near the top ten on a mountain-top finish but I was so determined to keep my form rolling along that I gave it everything. I had one final effort left in me up the final climb and the other riders in the breakaway began to fall away. I had broken them, went over the top in second place and held on for the descent to claim one of the greatest second-place finishes of my career. I was so exhausted afterwards that I virtually collapsed on my bike.

After the Vuelta, the world championships in Verona, Italy, were just around the corner and my name started being thrown around as one of the favourites. Again, I had a fantastic race, finishing fourth behind Oscar Freire, Erik Zabel and Luca Paolini, while teammate Allan Davis was fifth, which was a bit frustrating because I would have preferred one of us to get a medal but we didn't communicate well enough in the final. I attacked up the last climb but was caught just before the finish and our team hadn't spoken about what would happen if two of us came to the finish together. We both missed out on being world champion by one bike length.

I could have quite easily retired at the end of 2004, believing I'd achieved everything I'd aimed for. I had stood on the podium in the Classics, won stages of the Tour de

France, wore the yellow and green jersey, and now had an Olympic gold medal. I could have hung up the wheels and been happy.

CHAPTER 12

NO TEAM TO DREAM TEAM

Any Olympic year ends with a sense of relief. It's such a big build-up, more so emotionally because of all the pressure and stress, so I needed at least a month to recharge at the end of the 2004 season. But when you come off a year like that—when you've ticked a couple of boxes that you'd only dreamed of—it's hard to find new objectives. So suddenly there was even more pressure. I was being paid well and the team expected the big results to keep coming, but to be honest I thought I'd struggle to top what I'd achieved in 2004.

I wanted to kick off the year with a bang. I was third overall at the Tour Down Under behind winner Luis Leon Sanchez, who attacked on the Willunga Hill stage. Then I took my form to Europe where I had an okay Classics

STUART O'GRADY

campaign but it was nothing special. My best performance was fourth at Milan–San Remo, which was a great start, but after that nothing really went my way. I was tenth at Gent–Wevelgem, eleventh at E3 Prijs Vlaanderen, sixteenth at Tour of Flanders and eighteenth at Paris–Roubaix.

If nothing else, my results showed my consistency. But it was frustrating because while I was up there for every race, when Whitey (Matt White) exploded after working so hard for me, I was left isolated without any other teammates. And having that support in the final is the key to success in these races because you cannot win them on your own.

Immediately following the cobbled Classics are the Ardennes, three epic races within a week of each other: Amstel Gold, Fleche Wallonne and Liège-Bastogne-Liège. I rode some of the Ardennes in the early years of my career but after a while it got too difficult. I found that after Roubaix my body was wrecked, and mentally I was knackered. A new wave of riders comes through for the Ardennes, all the punchy little climbers who didn't ride the cobbles, and they'd been doing a different preparation in Spain. So if you rocked up to the Ardennes after racing Milan–San Remo, Tour of Flanders and Paris–Roubaix you'd be smashed before you even knew what was happening.

I wasn't meant to ride the Giro d'Italia that year but during my break after the cobbled Classics I was at home looking at the Giro's stage profiles. I noticed there was a 1 km prologue to start the race, which was pretty much the shortest prologue in history. I thought it would be cool to have a go at it so I conjured up this idea of riding it with a fixed gear on what was basically a track bike. I usually avoided the Giro d'Italia because it meant you wouldn't get a break after the Classics, but this year I thought I could do the 1 km prologue and contest a few sprints in the first two weeks, then go home.

So I called the boss and told him I wanted in on the Giro and I wanted a special bike for the prologue, no messing around with gears, no rear brake and I wanted double disc wheels. He was surprised but he agreed and I rocked up to the prologue with a time-trial bike, modified with a light-weight carbon seat, a fixed gear and missing everything we didn't think we'd need to get through a 1 km sprint.

The prologue went well and I was spot on with my gear choice, but after the finish line there was a barrier where you had to turn right. There was no way I could stop with only a front brake, so I had to make sure the masseur was there to catch me. I eventually finished sixth, 0.2 of a second behind the winner, fellow Aussie Brett Lancaster, who did an incredible ride. As agreed with the team, I stayed for the first two weeks and managed third on Stage 10 and sixth on Stage 2, but guys like Alessandro Petacchi were a step ahead. My best outcome at the Giro that year was abandoning mid-way through, jumping in a hire car with Baden Cooke and racing back to Monaco for the F1 Grand Prix, which we made just in time.

In July I went to the Tour de France where I was Mr Consistency with seven top-tens, eventually finishing second in the points classification for the green jersey amid plenty of drama.

Stage 3 was 212.5 km from La Châtaigneraie to Tours
but the fireworks went off in the final 100 metres when I
clashed with fellow Aussie sprinter, Robbie McEwen. The
incident saw Robbie relegated to the back of the field and
generated a media storm because the photos were pretty
graphic. As we approached the finish line I was in the
perfect position behind Tom Boonen. It's a real scrappy
sprint, just mayhem; you're hitting guys, locking up the
brakes, guys are dive-bombing underneath you and it's a
full-on fight. The next thing I realise, Robbie is right next
to me, trying to take my spot but I wasn't going to let him in
because there's no room for friends in a sprint. Of course
I stuck my elbow as far as I could into his ribcage and over
his arm, trying to block him because he was leaning over
and his head was right in my ribcage. There's so much
going on in a sprint and we had no intention of crashing
each other or inflicting any harm, it was just a ding-dong
battle—which is what makes sprinting such an adrenaline
rush. Robbie unleashed three pretty big head-butts on me
during the run to the finish. It was nothing I hadn't been
hit with before but three big ones can be a little excessive.

Afterwards I heard Robbie had been disqualified. Was
I surprised? No. Was I sad for him? No. Boonen won the
stage, I was third and Robbie was relegated to last place
which basically ended his hopes of winning the green
jersey that year. From that perspective I was sorry, but if I
hadn't been strong enough to hold him off in the sprint, I
would have been in the back of an ambulance.

It took a little while for us both to calm down after the

incident. I found Robbie at the start the next day and asked him what the hell he was thinking; it was over the top. He argued that it was my fault, but clearly the photos and video of the incident speak for themselves. Nevertheless, we never got angry at each other. I was just surprised that someone with his experience, and with the consequences that would follow, took it that far. But the show rolled on and many more battles lay ahead.

Later that year I decided not to ride the world titles in Madrid because I felt that I couldn't sacrifice myself for him after everything that had happened. But that was about as personal as our so-called feud ever got.

Robbie and I have had an interesting relationship over the years. There have been times I've wanted to throttle him, but I've always had the utmost respect for him. What he achieved on the bike was incredible. My respect for him was evident at the 2002 world championships in Zolder when he was second. I was right next to him, trying to shepherd him to the finish line and do everything I could to look after him, and he won Australia's first ever medal at a world titles.

From Robbie's point of view, I was never as fast as him but I could position myself well, which probably pissed him off because I'd be taking up the spot he might have wanted. Furthermore, he knew he was quicker than me which only fuelled the rivalry.

We've all said things in the heat of the moment that we ultimately regret, but it's hard because when you cross the finish line at 100 miles per hour, you're angry, on the verge of crashing, the adrenaline is rushing and your body is screaming with pain. Everything is chaos. Then suddenly journalists are sticking microphones in your face and, with the benefit of hindsight, you say things that you probably shouldn't.

As the years went on, I moved away from sprinting to focus on the Classics and consequently, there was no rivalry with Robbie anymore and we became pretty good friends. I'm really proud of what Robbie achieved in his career and we've been professional and manly enough not to become enemies. On the contrary, we have maintained a good relationship.

McEwen—three-time Tour de France green jersey winner—says in the early years he and Stuart were two young professionals 'pretty much going in the same direction and having a lot of the same goals'.

'We were both up there in the sprints and often we were in very close quarters, in the same place at the same time,' McEwen says. 'Then even on the domestic scene we'd be against each other in a crit series or a Sun Tour. Some of the frustration probably came from the fact that we were up there trying to be the best in the world, yet it was already hard enough trying to be the best Australian. There was definitely a big rivalry between us because being the best meant trying to beat each other.

'But the trick is leaving that aggression and cut-throat attitude out on the road. We've had a rocky relationship, got on great at times, not very well at other times, and purely because we're such competitive people.'

McEwen's recollection of the clash on Stage 3 of the 2005 Tour de France is as follows: 'I was trying to go forward one way while Stuey was trying to maintain position and go the other way. He got his elbow on top of my arm and I was trying to push him off it. I wasn't pissed at Stuey, I was pissed at the commissaires. It was a racing incident and I was pissed that I didn't win the stage and that I got disqualified. It annoyed me for the rest of the race and I lost the green jersey but I never saw it as a personal thing.'

As the pair ended their careers riding side by side at Orica-GreenEDGE, McEwen says that, above all, he and Stuart have the utmost respect for each other. 'He's done it all: as a track rider with the team pursuit and Olympic madison champion, on the road with wins in the Tour de France. He's stood on the podium of every Classic in his realm; his versatility, his doggedness and his fighting spirit are incredible.'

Towards the end of the 2005 season I felt like the flame had gone out. I realised that to rise to a new level, I needed a change. I had just done two years of super-hard work, carrying the team through every Classic and every race I started, and it was taking its toll. Okay, I went to Cofidis wanting to lead a team and to have more opportunities at winning a Classic, but the Classics team was basically them employing me. I was it. A few of the guys did what they could but I needed more support in the final and the situation wasn't getting any better.

I wanted a fresh start, to go to a team with a strong squad behind me, because it was becoming my life's mission to win one of cycling's monuments—Tour of Flanders, Paris–Roubaix, Milan–San Remo or Liège-Bastogne-Liège. So I set up a meeting with Giancarlo Ferretti who was in charge of the Fassa Bortolo team for many years. The godfather of Italian cycling, he was one of the most renowned managers of all time and had a very successful team, bringing up Alessandro Petacchi and Mario Cipollini. I met with him in September while I was in Italy visiting my sister who was living there at the time. I was pretty nervous because I'd heard many stories about him being such a hard bastard. Lesley, being the nice person she is, laid on a spread of cheese and chips—and the first thing Giancarlo said when he walked in was, 'O'Grady, no chips for you.' I thought, 'Holy shit, I can't even eat potato chips, I guess a beer is out of the question!' But the meeting went quite well and he basically gave me a contract on the spot for a new team which was to be sponsored by Sony Ericsson. It was a big contract for two or three years with big bonuses, so when he drove out the driveway a couple of hours later I was rapt.

I flew home to Australia for the start of summer then went to Fiji for a friend's wedding with Anne-Marie and

Seth. We visited a little island where I remember lying in a hammock and literally pinching myself. Here I was, in one of the most beautiful places in the world, parked on the beach, thinking about everything that had happened over the last few years, and contemplating my future with Mr Ferretti's team.

After a couple of days I turned on my phone to make sure there weren't any emergencies, but then about fifteen messages came through. From Rok: 'Ring me, urgent.' From a mate in Monaco: 'Stuart, please call, urgent, urgent.' I started freaking out so I called Rok and he told me that Sony Ericsson wasn't coming on board, the team wasn't folding, it just never existed in the first place and Mr Ferretti had been had.

I couldn't believe what I was hearing: here I was on a deserted island in December and I didn't have a team, which meant I didn't have a job for next season. To say that my holiday was ruined is an understatement. When I got back to Australia it was full panic mode. I'd gone from riding this beautiful wave to thinking, 'What the hell am I going to do?' When I got back to Adelaide I sat down with Anne-Marie and friend Paul Neighbour who has always been very influential in my life, particularly when it comes to financial decisions. I'm a bike-rider, not a businessman.

Paul put it really simply when he said, 'Forget money. If you had to ride for free, what is the one team you'd want to ride for to help you win a Classic?' And I replied, 'Well, there's only one: CSC with Bjarne Riis.'

I'd had enough frustrations and wanted to be a part

of a real team. I'd watched CSC for many years and they looked like the dream team. They won races left, right and centre; they rode past you in the peloton as one unit and they even looked cool, they looked classy. You'd be sitting at the dinner table in a hotel and they would be all laughing and loving life, then would go and rip us a new one in a race the following day. Jens Voigt, Bobby Julich, Kurt Asle Arvesen, Karsten Kroon, Marcus Lingqvist, Fabian Cancellara, the Schlecks, Carlos Sastre, Dave Zabriskie, Christian Vande Velde—the list went on and on.

Soon after I started getting messages from Patty Jonker who said, 'Mate, ring Bjarne.' But I didn't know Bjarne from a bar of soap, so I put it off. At the same time I was getting desperate, which is not a good position to be in when you're used to negotiating the best possible contract. But I was in no position to negotiate—I needed a team no matter what the price.

Soon after, a guy I had on the ground in Europe helping me out rang through with some good news: Team Unibet had come good with a big offer; in fact, it wasn't far off what I thought I'd be getting with Mr Ferretti. I was so relieved, but strangely I still wasn't happy because I knew that riding for Unibet would have been like going back to Cofidis. It would have been good money, but they didn't have anyone for the Classics and I would have found myself battling it out on my own for another top-twenty finish. So, after days of procrastinating, I decided to ring Bjarne. I felt he had to hear from me directly, not from someone else.

He was in the middle of lunch when I called and told me

he'd call back. When he did, the phone didn't even have time to ring, I was like, 'Yep, hi Bjarne.'

Bjarne is a very different person to talk to. He speaks very slowly and analyses everything that comes out of his mouth. He loves long, silent pauses which cracked most people in negotiations, but I just said, 'Look Bjarne, I want to come to your team.' This opened me up to being paid peanuts but I didn't have time to mess around and I was prepared to cop a hiding in the negotiating room.

He said he possibly had one position left on his team and I made it pretty clear that I didn't want to miss out. I knew that if I wanted to win a big race, this was the team for me. Deep down, I also knew that going to Unibet would only be a short-term monetary solution but I was heading into possibly the last two years of my career. So I said to Bjarne, 'How about you come back to me tomorrow with a figure that you're prepared to pay?' So the ball was in his court. When I hung up, I felt even more relieved than when I got the offer from Unibet. Bjarne knew about the offer from Unibet but the fact that I was willing to take a hit in the hip pocket to join his team showed my desire to win a Classic. There was no bullshit.

Paul Neighbour says Stuart brokering a deal with CSC reminded him of an episode of *The Simpsons*. 'Homer is trying to sell something and he says, "Before we start negotiating, I want you to know that I'm desperate and I'll take any offer."'

Throughout Stuart's career, Neighbour encouraged him to do his own negotiating so he knew exactly what was going on. 'That summer he came over and plonked himself down on the chair, he was pretty flat,' Neighbour recalls. 'The lifeline with Unibet was really good money and he said, "I think that's what I'll do."

'But I could tell he wasn't excited about the decision. So I questioned the decision, trying to discuss the other options and he said there weren't any. I suspected he meant in terms of money as a key rider in a pro team, but not necessarily as a cyclist. So I asked him, "Are you ready to finish cycling? Are you excited about bike-racing or is this just work now? Is it just about the money?" This stopped him in his tracks, I could see the cogs ticking over. I said, "Do you still want to win and if so, is Unibet going to give you the best chance to do that?"

'He told me it certainly wasn't and he would miss most of the key races he wanted to race. "So if you could ride for any team, who would it be?" I asked him.

'He replied, "CSC but that's just not an option". But for the first time I noticed the thought creeping into his mind that maybe this was it for his cycling career, and he may not ride for much longer. I think he got real motivation from that perspective.

'I said that I bet it was an option [to ride in team CSC] if you rang Bjarne and said you would ride on a basic domestique's salary. He did, he was riding now for his cycling career, he won Paris–Roubaix and the rest is history.'

The day after calling Bjarne I was pacing up and down the hallway when he rang with a figure. I nearly choked on the phone. I said, 'Mate, I know I said you could screw me over, but come on.' It was less than one-third of what Unibet had offered and it shocked me. But eventually I managed to get another 50,000 Euros out of him and the deal was done. In hindsight I could have gone for 100,000 Euros extra but didn't want to push my luck. I knew it was the right decision and I didn't give a shit about the money because at that stage of my career I would have ridden for nothing. Paul made me realise that what I wanted most in life was to win a Classic, no matter the price. I've never been big on money, it's a nice thing to have but I've never been obsessed by it. I've been able to do what I love and get paid for it.

I was relieved to be joining Bjarne and wanted to start with all guns blazing. Yet I also knew that I was going to a team that already had Fabian Cancellara. Although he was yet to win a Classic, he would be our leader in the big one-day races and go on to become one of the greatest Classics riders of our generation. But I looked at it as a positive and thought it could work in my favour. Fabian had been such a big hitter in the Classics; not only could I be there to support him, I knew the team would have four or five riders still there in the final when the race was won and lost. And that opened up a whole new opportunity for me to attack and have a crack for myself.

But just as the excitement grew for the Classics, I crashed during Tirreno–Adriatico. I had already missed the national titles and Tour Down Under to attend training camps; now here I was, at one of my first races with my new team and I hit a hole the size of a small car at 60 km/h. I snapped my forks, the handlebars punched straight through my chest and I snapped my collarbone and seven ribs. So in one crash my Classics campaign was over.

I had mixed emotions watching Fabian win Paris–Roubaix that year from my couch. I was devastated not to be there, but I was also so inspired. I was straight on the phone wanting to be part of the celebrations. My point had been proven—I was in a team that was capable of winning these big races so I felt I was a step closer to realising my dream.

I recovered in time for the Dauphine but bad luck managed to find me again at the Tour de France when I was taken out on the 216.5 km Stage 3 from Esch-sur-Alzette in Luxembourg to Valkenburg in the Netherlands. We were flying on a downhill when someone in front of me took my front wheel out with him. We were doing 60 km/h and as I looked up I saw a big steel pole with a road sign coming at me and there was nothing I could do. I smashed straight into it and when I got up there was a cracking pain in my back but I got on my bike and managed to finish the stage in all sorts of trouble. That night I had X-rays which showed a hairline fracture in one of my vertebrae. It was a tough gig but I decided to ride on and finish the Tour de France even though at times over the next seventeen stages I was in excruciating pain.

I don't think I've ever felt that consistently shit for so

long. On the team I felt like a third leg because every morning we'd talk tactics on the bus and the director would look at me and say, 'And Stuey, you just try to get to the finish again.' The boys helped me out, especially the day after the crash, because it started on a mountain and they pushed me up.

I felt better as the Tour went on. I got a lot of respect from the boys and was able to do my fair share of work in the latter stages. I rank getting to Paris that year as one of my greatest achievements on the bike.

One day I will never forget was being in that famous break-away on Stage 17 from Saint-Jean-de-Maurienne to Morzine when Floyd Landis attacked us on his own, 128 km from the finish. It was the first day after the crash that I started to feel good and I managed to get in the breakaway on the mountainous stage. There were thirteen guys in the breakaway and we were ten minutes up the road from the peloton when we heard over the radio that Landis was coming.

Normally with a break that size the race would be won by someone in the group, but not today. 'So who's he coming with?' I asked our team director over the radio. 'He's on his own,' he replied. 'What the hell? He's on his own? As if he's going to catch thirteen blokes!'

If I hadn't been in that breakaway that day I would never have believed it. We were watching the time board come down—nine minutes, eight minutes, seven minutes, six minutes—and everyone started getting nervous and eating and drinking. We were looking behind us waiting for Floyd to come past on a motorbike when, sure enough, he caught us. He turned to me and said, 'Stuey, hang on,' and off we went. I tried to hold onto his wheel for as long as possible but he blew everyone out the door. I was the second-last one to get dropped and was with a lot of good climbers while Floyd went on to win the stage by a whopping 5 minutes 23 seconds and in doing so, sealed overall victory.

Later on we found out the truth. Floyd wasn't racing clean, but I knew at the time that what he did that day wasn't normal.

Having ridden the Tour de France that year basically as a training ride while I recovered from my back injury, I came out feeling okay. The team wanted me to do a world cup race in Switzerland called Grand Prix Zurich. It was a super-hard hilly race, right up there with Tour of Flanders and Liège-Bastogne-Liège, and I asked the boss if I could skip it because it was just too hard for me at that time. But he said, 'Come on, you're really important for the team, we need your motivation for the boys even if it's just for 150 km.' So I agreed to race.

I remember sitting down the night before with Jens Voigt, Karsten Kroon, the Schlecks and Fabian. They were a team of absolute kickers and were all so pumped for this race. Their motivation gave me a huge lift so when I got the start line, bang, we were off and I found myself in the breakaway with Fabian.

Racing in his home country, he sacrificed himself for me 100 per cent that day. He made it possible for me to sprint to second place behind Samuel Sanchez. I thought, 'Holy

eur de PARIS-ROUBAIX 2007

© Graham Watson

Pure joy and relief – a lifetime of hard work pays off when Stuart hoists the 2007 Paris–Roubaix trophy above his head after becoming the first Australian to win the one-day Classic.

Celebrating winning the inaugural Tour Down Under in 1999.

Lance Armstrong leads Stuart and Davide Vigano on stage three of the 2011 Tour Down Under.

Stuart leads team Leopard-Trek in training for the Tour Down Under.

…eading an escape with Simon Gerrans (far right) on stage two of the Tour Down Under.

…lan Davis and Stuart on stage four of the Tour Down Under.

…tuart wins a stage of the Tour Down Under in Victor Harbor.

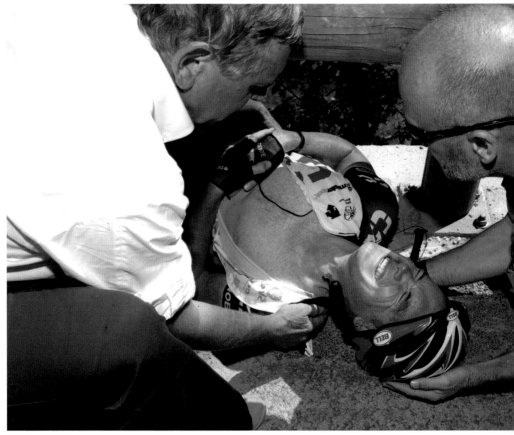

Stuart crashes on the descent of the Cormet de Roselend on stage eight of the 2007 Tour de France.

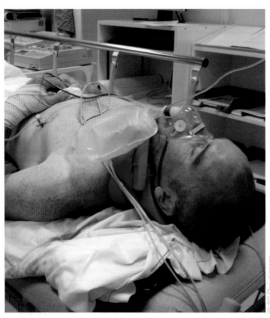

© BS Christiansen

Lying in hospital after his 2007 crash.

A crash early in the 2008 Giro d'Italia left Stuart with a broken collarbone.

...tuart goes flying over the handlebars during the Tour of California.

...he aftermath of the crash.

Stuart with his father Brian in Stuart's team-issued GAN colours.

Stuart and good friend Jay Sweet on a training ride.

Stuart with GAN teammate Chris Boardman.

Joking with cycling commentator Phil Liggett at the Tour Down Under.

Stuart with team director Matt White and teammate Robbie McEwen at the 2012 Tour Down Under.

Andy Schleck and Stuart riding together in the 2012 Tour of Oman.

© Graham Watson

tuart with Aussie sprinter Matt Goss during the 2011 Tour e Suisse.

Celebrating with Thomas Rohregger after teammate Daniele Bennati won a stage of the 2011 Vuelta a Espana.

tuart (left) with Carlos Sastre in the yellow jersey riding onto the hamps Elysees in the 2008 Tour de France.

With good friend and former teammate David Millar in the Tour de France.

tuart being taken back to the team bus by good friend John evorrow after a stage of the 2008 Tour de France.

With fellow Australian Allan Davis before a stage of the Tour Down Under.

Stuart celebrates winning the 2007 Paris-Roubaix with son, Seth.

Wearing the green jersey with parents Brian and Fay before a stage of the Tour de France in the late 90s.

Stuart celebrates winning the 2003 national championship with father Brian and wife Anne-Marie.

shit, this guy has just helped me get second in a world cup on his home turf!' He got a lot of respect from me that day. It showed me his level of commitment and the sacrifice guys on this team were prepared to make for each other. It marked the start of something very special, and from then on we became inseparable. We roomed together at every race and helped each other win a lot of big races. He even flew me to his home city of Bern on a private jet after the 2011 Milan–San Remo (where he came second behind Australian Matt Goss) to celebrate his thirtieth birthday.

Fabian Cancellara said the only thing he knew about Stuart before they became teammates at CSC was that he was 'a great rider with blonde hair'. They met on a pre-season training camp in Denmark and soon realised they had a connection, but they didn't do a lot of racing together until the 2006 Vuelta a España when they won the team time-trial and then Grand Prix Zurich.

'It was shit weather, raining all day, and I wasn't the guy to go for team leadership that day,' Cancellara says. 'Then suddenly I was in the break with Stuey. I was so dead but I sacrificed myself from the bottom of the downhill until the last kilometre— everything that day was for him and after that our friendship started.'

But according to Cancellara, their friendship went well beyond the bike and included Stuart teaching him to speak English. 'I learnt a lot from him about leadership, about taking the pain out on yourself and going fully in. He taught me that pain is temporary, but memories are forever.

'He now lives in Luxembourg and we are busy. But I know that when I need someone, when I have a problem, whatever it is, Stuey will help me and be there for me. We have something from the past that will not go away.'

CHAPTER 13

A BEAUTIFUL DAY

The night before 2007 Paris–Roubaix, Fabian and I sat in our hotel room in Compiègne and watched a replay of him winning the race the year before. Fabian was pretty big on looking at videos of old races; it was part of his pre-race motivation, though not something I would do that often. Fabian would even watch races that he didn't win, just in case he could learn something from them, so being his roommate that week we watched footage of three or four different Paris–Roubaixes. It's a bit like a Formula One driver memorising a circuit in his head. Obviously we can't memorise all 260 km of roads and cobbles, but there are pivotal moments in the race where you have to be at the front to either inflict damage or avoid it. So we'd sit and talk tactics for hours, discussing different race plans or the perfect scenario. I guess other riders were doing the same thing in their rooms, but we certainly didn't leave any stone unturned in our preparation.

As we sat there watching the replay of Fabian winning his first Paris–Roubaix trophy, we were interrupted by a knock on the door. Our sports director, Scott Sunderland, walked in. 'Boys,' he said, 'it's going to be 27 degrees tomorrow. Stuey, this is right up your alley.' He wasn't trying to undermine Fabian's role as team leader, but he said, 'Look mate, we've got to be prepared for anything to happen out there because a lot of Europeans are going to suffer.' At that moment, I don't think I've ever been as excited before a race in my entire life. I just had an inkling that maybe tomorrow might be my day because even Mother Nature was on my side. It had been the warmest period in Europe for many years, with sunshine replacing the usual wet, cold, gloomy conditions of Paris–Roubaix. I always performed well in hot weather, perhaps because I had thirty-four Australian summers in me, whereas Fabian was the opposite.

My lead-in form was pretty good. During pre-season I went to one of CSC's famous training camps which involved a hell of a lot of bike-riding. It was two weeks of intervals, hill climbing, race simulation, sprints and everything in between. We'd do 120 km in the morning on road bikes then swap over for 120 km on the time-trial bikes in the afternoon, which was unheard of in any other team that I knew of.

I went from the training camp to the Tour of California in February where I finished fifth overall. This really kick-started my season and I went to Europe with a lot of confidence. I was now in my second year with the team, we were riding well together and had so many big-hitters that we could control every race we went to. It was a lot of fun. Instead of being the guy on another team saying, 'Wow, there's CSC,' now I was in that very train. We took every race super-seriously and aimed to win every one we started.

I was fourth in Milano–Torrino, had really good form in Tirreno–Adriatico and managed to get over a couple of quite hard mountain days to finish fourteenth overall. Then I was fifth in the first big Belgian classic, Het Volk. I was fifth in Milan–San Remo and tenth in Tour of Flanders. For the first time I wasn't up there on my own; I'd turn around and there'd be Fabian Cancellara, Matti Breschel and Lars Michaelsen right next to me. I knew we had a super-strong team.

In the build-up to Paris–Roubaix, all the pressure was on Fabian. He was the defending champion who rode solo to victory in 2006 and the outright favourite to win again. I was still feeling pretty fresh; my tenth place in Flanders involved a lot of work for Fabian and yet I was still up there in the final so my confidence was high. In every race that spring, I went back to the team bus and knew deep down that my form was awesome. And while Fabian was the favourite to win Paris–Roubaix, there was no pressure at all on me. No one would have even mentioned my name that week, which was fine by me.

For two weeks during the spring Classics our team would be based in a hotel in the Belgian city of Kortrijk in West

Flanders. It became our home away from home where we formed our own family and experienced so much together. And we knew that after Paris–Roubaix on the Sunday night, we'd be on holiday.

The week of Paris–Roubaix we raced Gent–Wevelgem on the Wednesday, did 120 km of reconnaissance over most of the cobbled sections on Thursday, then on Friday we rode the 80 km into Compiègne. Saturday is all about the food—it's about eating until you can no longer fit one more piece of penne in your mouth. It starts with breakfast—oatmeal, ham and cheese omelette, a baguette and a couple of coffees to kick-start the engine. Then lunch—absolutely no salad, a piece of lettuce is not going to help you the next day, you've got to stock the engine with pasta, rice and chicken. We snack in between and dinner is two proper plates of pasta or rice, a steak, vegetables to help it all go down and a French apple pie because when you get to the line in the morning, you've got to have the tank on full.

At the team meeting on Saturday night, it was decided that we should have two men in the breakaway. Fabian—the raging favourite—would sit in the bunch on cruise control with a designated teammate in front of him the entire time, blocking the wind or helping in case he crashed or punctured. Luke Roberts and Matti Breschel's job was to make sure a break didn't go up the road without us being represented. It was like a chess game: putting riders out the front knowing that their day might be over after 200 km but they would have done their job. My job was to be up there at the start, make sure we had one or two guys on the front so we didn't miss the break, then go in the last wave of attacks before Fabian when the race reached the pointy end.

Regardless of the weather, anything can happen when you're racing on cobbles. Some of these roads are only open for one day of the year; the rest of the time they're used by farmers and their tractors. The Arenberg forest is a historical site only open to the public for this iconic bike race. With such rough terrain, your bike has got to be able to handle a thrashing and the bikes for Paris–Roubaix are especially built to be one centimetre longer in the frame so the rake is a little bit smoother and you get a more comfortable ride over the cobbles. We have special wheels and 28 mm tyres, which are like tractor tyres compared to what we normally race on, and they have a lot less air pressure. That day I had five-and-a-half bar (79psi) in the front and five bar in the back and usually we race on 10–12 bar.

The night before the race, a few mechanics who usually work on MotoGP bikes came over from Italy to prepare Fabian's and my bikes; no one knew except us and a few people on the team. The mechanics used a special low-friction lubricant on every moving part of the bike. As the centre bracket and the bearings in the hubs heated up, they became less resistant, and where the lubricant heats up the molecules create less friction so everything is spinning a lot quicker. It was the first time I was privileged enough to have these guys come in to help me. It was all new and freaky to me, the mechanics were walking around in a sealed room with masks and gloves in what looked like an operating theatre. It was a lot of effort for a bike that is done and dusted after one race, but that year it would prove well and truly worth it.

International cycling commentator Phil Liggett is widely known as the voice of cycling, having been given a front-row seat to the sport's biggest races for over forty years. According to Liggett, the only way to describe Paris–Roubaix is 'hell on wheels'.

'The roads were built in the sixteenth and seventeenth centuries and they're pretty much left the way they were,' Liggett says. 'Unless you ride Paris–Roubaix, even on a touring ride, you can't really appreciate it. Riding those stones is quite bloody ridiculous and once you start struggling and slipping in the cracks, you're as good as dead. For days afterwards your body is still humming, it's still vibrating from all those cobbles. You've got sores on the palm of your hands and on your fingers.

'Bernard Hinault said it best. He told organisers he rode it to win it so he could tell them they'd never see him ride it again—and that's exactly what he did.'

Stuart's brother Darren was given a unique insight into Paris–Roubaix in the late 1990s when he travelled to the race as a guest of Stuart's then team, GAN. 'Standing in the Arenberg forest, as anyone will tell you, it seems impossible for a push-bike to pass through. Motorbikes collapse, suspension systems break, cars get flat tyres—yet bike-riders somehow come flying through,' he says.

On race day we were up at 7 am. I looked out the hotel room window to see clear, blue skies. I grabbed Fabian's portable speaker, which cranked out some serious decibels, and put on U2's 'Beautiful Day'—which in hindsight was an omen for how the day would pan out. We were so pumped, how I imagine footballers must feel on the morning of a grand final.

The start was mayhem as usual with huge crowds there to see us off. I remember feeling so relaxed and confident; I had done everything right—I'd been training for months, done all the preparation races and I was fit and healthy. I didn't want to be signing autographs or talking to any more journalists, I just wanted to pin on my number and race. We had one final debrief in the team bus to go over everyone's roles and I said to the boys, 'If I win this race, first of all I'm going to take you to Ibiza for a party, then I'll be happy to retire.'

The race started mad fast as it always does. Ninety per cent of the peloton would love to be in the morning break-away because you're first into the cobbles and there's no fighting for position.

From experience, I know pretty much where the break

is going to go. Each year, it's on one of the small climbs after about 40 km because everyone has gone mental for the first hour and they're starting to get tired. So I started poking my nose up the front when suddenly a group went away. Matti Breschel was in it, and Luke Roberts was going up with another group. Normally eight, ten or twelve riders maximum would be allowed to go in a breakaway but this day it was huge. Then a rider in front of me attacked so I jumped on his wheel, turned around and saw we had a gap on the bunch which had pretty much sat up. I sprinted across to the front guys and that was it, the break was done and I was in it with two teammates and thirty other riders. I thought, 'This is unbelievable,' so straight away I told Luke to get on the front and work as hard as he could to keep this break moving.

We motored along at 50 km/h and I started yelling at everyone in the break, 'Come on guys, this is perfect, this is awesome, let's get as far as we can!' They were like a big bunch of sheep: willing to listen to anyone. A lot of guys, especially the younger ones, tend to wait for their director to tell them what to do, but it takes a long time to relay back to the team cars which numbers are in the front group. They use a lot of effort to get in the break then think, 'Shit, what do I do now? Sit in or work?' So I tried to get in their heads and gee them up before their director told them otherwise. It's about keeping the guys motivated, telling them that the further we go, the better it is for them and their leader.

So we're humming along but I hadn't even gone near

the front; I was sitting at the back yelling at blokes. That's the beauty of having teammates in the breakaway because Luke and Matti really kept the pressure on and after 115 km we had a gap of 4 minutes 30 seconds. All the big teams were represented in the break and I clearly remember thinking, 'This is absolutely perfect, these guys are towing me to the finish.' I felt more confident than I'd ever felt before.

As we approached the first cobbled section, a 2.2 km stretch known as Troisvilles à Inchy, I decided I wanted to go in first. Milram's Ralf Grabsch attacked the breakaway and ended up leading by about one minute by the time we got to the 2.4 km-long Arenberg forest, the heartbeat of Paris–Roubaix. But I didn't care because it was a ridiculous move made way too early. All I wanted was to conserve energy.

But just as we cruised into the Arenberg—bang, I got a puncture. I'd done everything perfectly then felt the vibrations through my spine, my eyeballs were rattling in my head and my back wheel was sliding around like I was on an ice-rink. I knew we had spare wheels at the end of the section but that was at least 1 km away. I parked on the right-hand side of the cobbles and thought, 'That's it, it's all over.' I was absolutely devastated because I knew the team cars were a long way behind. As I ripped my back wheel out, a support motorbike drove by and gave me a Mavic wheel. It was handy but it didn't really go well with our equipment, so I had to ride with a dodgy rear wheel as I watched my breakaway companions ride off into the dust.

I'd lost about a minute and a half, but what I did here was crucial to setting me up later on. In my younger days I would have time-trialled my way back to the breakaway, using all my energy on a long stretch of bitumen after the forest. But there was no way I could catch such a big group so I sat up, rolled along and ate everything that was in my pockets while I waited for the next group, which included Fabian and Tom Boonen. I was in no-man's land as I went through the next two sections—Wallers à Helesmes and Hornaing à Wandignies-Hamage—on my own but I could hear the chasing pack coming behind me.

When I was caught, I was pretty certain my race was done and dusted so as quickly as I could, I found Fabian and asked him how he was. He said he was okay, but I noticed a lot of salt marks all over his jersey and his shorts. Suddenly, Boonen's Quickstep boys attacked at full gas over the next section but I was straight onto them. I looked around at everyone—Juan Antonio Flecha, Leif Hoste, Boonen—and they looked shithouse. They'd been going bloody hard to bridge that five-minute gap to me for a long time while I'd been cruising in the breakaway and refuelling after the puncture.

Shortly afterwards, my group split again because when guys attacked on the next section they were going 100 per cent in a bid to blow the race to pieces. Our bunch was gradually dwindling, guys were crashing over water bottles that were like hand grenades on the road, but all the favourites were still together. At this point, our directors Scott and Bjarne told us to put the pressure on. It was my teammate Lars Michaelsen's last bike race after a long and fantastic career and he was on a mission, attacking his own shadow. He went away and ended up catching the front group so things were back in our favour.

Soon after, Scott told me to give it everything I had. Fabian was to attack, then ride across to Lars and the front group where he would fight it out for the win. As I went into the next section there was a left-hander where I was preparing to go full gas for Fabian. I don't know what went wrong because as I came into the cobbles my front wheel flew out from under me and before I knew it, I was on my arse.

It's got to be one of the quickest recoveries I've ever done because I jumped straight up and got back on my bike within five seconds. I had punctured in the forest and now crashed in the chase group so I was really angry. I used all my rage to go flat out across the cobbles and rode past guys who just minutes before had attacked me. Suddenly I was back with Fabian and Boonen.

I could see on their faces that they were cooked. Their jerseys were white from salt and mine was too, but I was handling the heat a lot better. I rode up next to Fabian and asked how he was. He looked at me and said, 'Not good. You go if you can.' Hearing those words was like floodgates bursting open. I finally had my chance.

As I was talking to Fabian I saw Steffen Wesemann attack on the right side of the road; immediately I was out of the saddle. There was so much dust and dirt that a lot of guys didn't see me go, and by the time they realised we'd attacked from the group, they had lost us. If you're not on the wheel when an attack goes in these big races, you don't want to waste energy chasing and towing everyone else along.

I tagged onto the back of Roger Hammond and Wesemann and just sat there because there was no one left, there was daylight between us and Boonen's group and I wasn't going to help because we still had Michaelsen and Breschel at the front of the race. Hammond and Wesemann were yelling at me to come and help them but there was no way I was putting in any effort to catch my teammates up the road. I just sat in while they drove us along at warp speed.

Because the breakaway had been going almost all day, it didn't take long to catch them and we re-grouped at the front. I knew Wesemann and Hammond had just done massive efforts—they'd basically done a time-trial to bring back the break—so as soon as we caught them I could see the guys drinking. As they slowed down they were spread across the road and we were flying towards them.

As soon as we tagged on the back, instinct kicked in. This was the moment. This was it. I had to go all-in. Everyone else in that group was nailed and I was still feeling okay.

Once I attacked, all my cards were laid bare. If it was a game of poker, I was all-in and there was no turning back. As I attacked I saw the '25 km to go' sign and thought, 'Holy shit, that's a long way to go on my own,' but I was committed and was out of the seat sprinting. That's when it hit me that I was leading Paris–Roubaix.

After the initial adrenaline of launching the attack subsided I was hoping the guys behind me would be disorganised and disoriented in all the dust and heat. So I decided to go at 90 per cent on the cobbles, then when I hit the bitumen I'd make the difference by going at 100 per cent effort. The gap was hovering around twenty seconds for a while and the time boards I was getting were so important because I thought, 'Am I going fast enough? Are they going to catch me?' I wanted to get the lead to one minute because if that happened, I could still have a puncture and win the race, but also, it would be a mental blow for the guys behind me. A one-minute lead would have done their heads in and they would have conceded that they were now racing for second and third.

I was paranoid coming through the Carrefore De L'Abre that some Belgian fan was going to wipe my head off with a giant flag. People were spraying champagne and beer on me but that didn't worry me; my only concern was being taken out by a spectator who'd been drinking in the sun all day.

I was trying to keep spinning the legs as much as possible because if you push a big gear you're more likely to cramp, but it was getting harder and harder. My arms were buckled and I was petrified about puncturing or having a mechanical problem. It was excruciating. Over the radio Scotty was saying, 'Mate, this is it, this is your day, you can win Paris–Roubaix!' I'd made it over the cobbles with my shabby back wheel still in place and that's when I honestly started to believe that I could win. I remember thinking, 'If

I get a puncture and lose this, I'm going to retire. I know this race is called the Hell of the North but any more bad luck would be just wrong.'

After the last section of cobbles there's a little rise in the road, not even a hill, but a gradual climb from 4 km to go to 3 km to go. I knew when I got over that, I had it won. My body was screaming at me to stop but my legs were going left, right, left, right, come on, I'm nearly there.

I knew Anne-Marie and Seth were in the Roubaix velodrome but I had no idea where. Throughout those last few kilometres of pain and torture, I was thinking, 'My God, my family is in that velodrome!' There were so many emotions going through me. But even then, I was worried about coming into the velodrome and sliding on the track because my tyres were so dusty so I took the last corner like an old grandpa. Then the crowd started roaring and it felt like I was being lifted off the ground. It was like watching the whole thing from a helicopter. There was so much relief; I'd been dreaming of winning one of these races my entire career, watched so much footage of Eddy Merckx, Sean Kelly, Franco Bellarini, Johan Museeuw and Tom Boonen winning in this velodrome. But you never think it will happen to you. A boy from Adelaide who grew up racing against his own stopwatch every night after school had just won Paris–Roubaix.

My victory salute was not going to be a wimpy, one-armed punch; it was about ten salutes rolled into one. Crossing the line I just collapsed, I couldn't pedal one more pedal-stroke and the guys pushed me to the podium. Everyone wants to slap you on the back and every slap feels like a Mike Tyson blow to the ribs. My body was cramping, I had dirt in my mouth and dust in my eyes.

I shed a tear when I finally saw Anne-Marie and Seth but one of the most emotional embraces that day was with Fabian. I was in the middle of an interview with a French television crew when mid-sentence Fabian came smashing his way through the crowd and got me in a giant bear hug, then grabbed my face with both hands and looked at me with such genuine joy. We'd gone to battle, and I know this phrase isn't used lightly but we were prepared to die for each other in these big races. Fabian nearly ripping my head off with happiness meant a bloody lot to me. There was no disappointment that he was the favourite and I had won.

As I climbed onto the podium I looked out over the crowd and saw some riders still coming into the velodrome looking over to see who had won. I had been one of those guys so many times and now I was the one they were all looking at. I was still wearing my bike shoes and nearly fell over when I hoisted the giant rock over my head. Of all the trophies you can get in world sport—flashy rings for a basketball championship, a silver cup for a tennis grand slam and a green jacket for a golf major—this was just a piece of rock but it was so significant. It shows that this is what you've raced over, it was your battlefield and here's a piece of it to remember forever.

Another Paris–Roubaix tradition is the shower block, which was part of the original velodrome that had been there for over a hundred years. They're ancient, concrete cubicles and most of the water is cold by the time you get in, but on every one is a tiny gold plaque engraved with the winner's name and year. It's a very special place; you can shower in Eddy Merckx's cubicle or any legend of the past.

But I didn't have time to shower there that night because I was whisked away to a media conference and doping controls. When I got back to the team bus the first person I saw was Whitey and we shared such a special moment. To have one of my oldest mates giving me the biggest hug meant so much. As I sat there with Seth over my shoulder, I was in another world, total disbelief.

Fabian Cancellara says the joy he felt was as if he'd won the race himself. 'For me it felt like I had won. I was not jealous, just proud of what we'd done. It was just a pleasure.'

For Anne-Marie, it was the first time she had seen Paris–Roubaix live. After flying to Brussels on the morning of the race, she and Seth spent the day in the team bus on their way to the velodrome in Roubaix. 'I was sitting in the team bus watching the race on TV and Seth was fast asleep on my lap,' Anne-Marie recalls. 'We soon realised Stu was out the front of the breakaway and that's when the reality started to set in that he could win. Seth was still sound asleep but with 15 km to go I had to wake him up and the team helped us get through the crowd and into the velodrome. I was standing there with Matt

White, so it was good to be with such a close friend to share the experience.

'I can't explain the feeling when Stu rode into the velodrome; I had goosebumps. To be there to see the people cheering—that's when you realise what an achievement it was. It was a beautiful day.'

While the final kilometres of the race were unfolding in Roubaix, on the other side of the world in Adelaide in the early hours of the morning, Stuart's parents Brian and Fay were glued to their computer waiting for constant updates.

'My first reaction was to say nothing, then as the finish got closer Fay was saying, "He's going to win this." And I said, "Shut up, don't say that."

'I shed a tear, I'm nearly shedding a tear now just thinking about it. It was not only that he'd won it, it was how he won it, in the classic road-race style.'

Phil Liggett says Stuart's effort to rejoin the breakaway after his puncture in the Arenberg forest was almost as impressive as his solo attack to win the race. 'He punctured, disappeared from the breakaway and we just crossed him off our list because nobody ever said he came back,' Liggett recalls of commentating that day.

'And out of the bloody fog and dust, I looked at Paul Sherwen and said, "That's O'Grady who's attacked." And Sherwen goes, "Where did he come from?"

Scott Sunderland remembers having a strange feeling of confidence in the days leading up to the race that Stuart could get the job done. 'I really felt that he was the horse we needed to back that day because if he was ever going to win a big Classic, that was the day. It was unusually hot and he was in great condition,' Sunderland says. 'When these opportunities come along and when that door is open, you've got to go through it.'

According to Sunderland, what made the victory so memorable for the team was Stuart's selfless attitude in the months leading into the race. 'The thing that stands out is how he laid everything on the line in every race—in Tirreno, in Flanders—all for Fabian,' he says. 'Even when he was in the front group of Paris–Roubaix, until I said to him, "Stuey, go, this is your chance," he was still riding for Fabian.

Luke Roberts was one of Stuart's teammates that day. The two share a special bond because they both come from Adelaide and emerged through the national track program.

Roberts says it was a 'special' moment to see his long-time friend achieve his ultimate dream.

'My job was done by the time we got to the second feed station at about the 200 km mark. I'd been dropped so I got in a car and we went straight to the velodrome. We saw him make his attack on the TV in the bus and once he was only a couple of kilometres away, we jumped out and ran into the velodrome to see the final lap.

'I was part of the team the year before when Fabian Cancellara won, but having known Stuey for so long, and knowing how much he loved that race, made it even more special. He's definitely one of the toughest characters in the sport; he's had some nasty crashes and always bounced back.'

The team decided to stay on in Kortrijk that night instead of flying home and we shared an incredible night. Lars Michaelsen—who'd been looking really good to get second place in the final race of his career—had a mechanical problem and crashed on the cobbles just before the finish. I could tell he was devastated but was doing his best to put on a happy face for the team; I really felt for him.

We had some really nice speeches for Lars' retirement, celebrating his commitment to the team, and I'll be forever grateful for what he did for me. I got up and said a few quiet words, called for quite a few champagne toasts, and kept looking down in front of me and seeing this great big bloody rock. So much goes on behind the scenes that I wanted to go around thanking each and every person on the team—whether it was the person who filled up the drink bottles, who made the food, who stood outside with spare wheels all day, or other riders who sacrificed their own hopes to help you achieve a lifelong dream. A couple of months later I bought them all a bottle of South Australia's finest wine, a Chris Ringland 2000 shiraz, formerly known as the Three Rivers Vineyard. I wanted to give these guys something special that originated from the roads where I began my career, the Barossa Valley. It was something they could put in their cellar and in twenty years' time crack it open and remember that special occasion when our team conquered the toughest one-day race in the world.

But no present—not even a top-shelf bottle of red wine—could express my gratitude. I remember thanking Bjarne a hundred times for giving me an opportunity I thought I'd never get, and we spoke about our phone conversations a couple of years earlier when I was without a team. I knew that to achieve my dreams I had to be on a team like his and those dreams had come true. It really was a beautiful day.

The following day, Stuart took his family to Disneyland, honouring a promise he'd made to Anne-Marie prior to the race. As she recalls, 'Before the race I said to Stu, "Why don't I come up to Paris–Roubaix and we can go to Disneyland with Seth the next day?" I was thinking that Fabian Cancellara was the favourite and Stu was working for him, so I figured he'd race that day then we'd go on a bit of a holiday.

'When he ended up winning, I said to him, "Don't worry about tomorrow, we don't need to go to Disneyland.' But he replied, "No, no, we'll still go."

'I was pregnant with Keira so I couldn't stay up late drinking champagne but the team had a well-deserved celebration. Then the next morning we're walking around Disneyland in disbelief that the day before he'd just won Paris–Roubaix. I think we celebrated by watching the Mickey Mouse parade. It was really special because he could have celebrated with the boys for days but he chose to spend the day with us.'

Vital statistics

105th Paris–Roubaix; Sunday, 15 April 2007
259 km from Compiègne to Roubaix; 28 cobbled sectors

Starters: 187

Finishers: 101

Team CSC: Stuart O'Grady, Fabian Cancellara, Lars Michaelsen, Matti Breschel, Marcus Ljungqvist, Kasper Klostergaard, Allan Johansen, Luke Roberts.

Top 5: Stuart O'Grady (CSC) 6hrs 9mins 7secs; Juan Antonio Flecha (Rabobank) and Steffen Wesemann (Wiesenhof Felt) +0.52; Bjorn Leukemans (Predictor-Lotto) +0.53; Roberto Petito (Liquigas) +0.55.

CHAPTER 14

MY OLD FRIEND, PAIN

This is how crazy cycling can be. One day you've won a monument and achieved everything you've ever dreamt of. Then three months later you're lying on the side of the road, almost dead.

I walked away from the 2007 Classics floating on a cloud after winning Paris–Roubaix. Every morning I'd wake up to see this rock sitting on the kitchen table; the first few mornings I went over and gave it a little tap and asked, 'How you doin'?' Coming away from that spring knowing I'd won the biggest race I could ever have imagined was surreal.

Eventually though, it was time to refocus and start training again. While riding around, people were stopping to congratulate me; I'd be introduced to people as 'the guy who just won Paris–Roubaix' and I heard people talking about my win as I walked past them.

The Tour de France was my next big aim. We had a pretty serious team with Carlos Sastre and Frank Schleck expected to contend for the GC (general classification) and it was my job to protect them. That year the race was to start in London with a 7.9 km prologue through the city.

I was really pumped for the prologue because I knew my form was good; also, rooming with Fabian automatically gets you motivated because you see how much effort he puts into his preparation and how much he analyses everything. So I tried to use his energy and expertise in that area by asking him about his gear ratios and other such things.

Of all my Tours de France, the crowd in London that day was the biggest I ever saw on the roadside; it was absolutely phenomenal. It was a beautiful day and I was pushing it to the limit, as you do in every prologue, and at the halfway mark I had the fastest time. Then there was a tricky chicane with a left-hand corner. As I came out of it, I let the bike drift a bit too far; I thought I had it under control but my back foot clipped the barrier and the next thing I knew I was sliding along the road on my bum. I got back on my bike and finished 179th behind Fabian, who blitzed everyone to win by thirteen seconds. It was frustrating, but mostly I was disappointed for the boys because we missed out on the teams classification by just two seconds to Astana because of my crash. I was lucky to avoid injury; I lost a few freckles and a bit of pride but it could have been worse.

Having won the prologue, Fabian took the yellow jersey,

which meant I was riding on the front for pretty much the entire first week. We did massive turns starting with a team time-trial for the first few kilometres of each stage to nullify any attempted attack. Then we'd slowly back the pace off, and because we had such a strong team we decided who and how many riders we'd let go in a breakaway. I did hundreds of kilometres on the front, which was a massive workload, but I was prepared for it because Bjarne told us we had the toughest job of the whole race—controlling the front, setting the pace running into the mountains then covering moves in the last week.

Fabian had just surrendered the yellow jersey to Linus Gerdemann when we began Stage 8 on Sunday 15 July. We faced a couple of major climbs on the relatively short stage of 165 km from Le Grand-Bornand to Tignes, and I knew I was on good form. Every Tour de France, I always have one day when I climb really well. I can never predict when it's going to be but there's always one stage each year when I think, 'Holy shit, I feel like a climber.' And so it was on Stage 8 that year.

I negotiated the first three climbs before we faced the first serious Category 1 ascent, the Cormet de Roseland, which was a fairly brutal 19 km climb with an average gradient of 6 per cent. By the time we got over the top there were only about thirty guys left in the front group and I was quite surprised to be there. The bunch had split and I was hanging on to the front group when Bjarne called me on the team radio to tell me to come back to the car to get water because it was important our riders had water bottles before the next mountain.

So I dropped back to the team car, filled up my jersey with eight water bottles and started descending at about 80–90 km/h to try to distribute them. By this stage everyone was riding in single file because of the speed of the descent. I was in the full tuck position to stay out of the wind when the guy in front of me—and to this day I don't know who it was—swung out to his right to miss a pothole as I was coming around him. Suddenly, his back wheel swiped my front one from right under me. I didn't even have time to blink; there was no way I could avoid it and I was sent catapulting through the air.

He rode off while I was flung to the left of my bike and slammed into a wooden post. Along with those eight water bottles stuffed down the back of my jersey that acted like an airbag around my spine, that pine post probably saved my life that day because without it, I would have gone hurtling over the edge of the mountain, free-falling God knows how many metres into a ravine, and probably to my death.

My body took most of the impact, but judging by my helmet which had cracked in half at the back, my head had wrapped around the post and I later found out I had a blood clot and bleeding on the brain. It was the scariest moment of my life. I couldn't feel my legs while literally metres away guys were riding past me at 80 km/h. All I could hear was 'whoosh, whoosh' of their tyres. I wanted to get out of the way but I couldn't. I had no sensation in my legs, which freaked me out big time. I tried to sit up but I couldn't. I couldn't even turn my head to look to the side. I was conscious throughout the whole ordeal so kept looking straight up into the sky when suddenly a circle of camera flashes appeared from everywhere. Then I heard the familiar voice of BS Christensen who was holding my hand telling me I'd be okay. BS was a member of the Danish military who worked with CSC and ran some of our pre-season camps; he was the first person from the team on the scene.

The pain was beyond comprehension. I've broken a lot of bones in my time, have even got up and finished bike races with broken collarbones, but this was different. This was internal and it wasn't just in one area; my whole body was an inferno of pain. I was terrified that I still couldn't get up because of the pain in my back, and I was in a panic, thinking, 'Am I paraplegic?'

There was water everywhere, and initially the onlookers had no idea where it had come from, but then they saw our team bottles scattered across the road. If it wasn't for the water bottles in my jersey protecting my spine, I don't know if I'd still be here. I could have snapped my spinal cord straight through.

The medicos had quite a lot of trouble getting me off the ground but eventually I was put into an ambulance on a stretcher and taken to hospital at the bottom of the Rose-land. I was injected with morphine, given an oxygen mask and then everything became a blur of noise and pain.

BS came to see me in hospital and said, 'Look, we're going to have to put you in a helicopter and get you out of here.' At that point I knew I was in some serious strife.

As I was loaded into the helicopter, I noticed I was wearing a neck brace and could only look straight up at the rotor blades. I'm not ashamed to say I was absolutely terrified. I started thinking about my family and what would happen if I couldn't walk again.

A new wave of panic set in when I arrived by chopper at Chambery Hospital because the doctors and nurses were rushing around everywhere, which told me I was either in a fair bit of trouble or they were just really keen to help out. I needed an MRI scan so they lifted me up and put me inside the machine, which has scarred me ever since. I was placed on a flat, hard surface and my back roared with pain. My nose was only a couple of inches off the surface and it felt like I was being put in a coffin. The MRI revealed that I had two broken shoulder blades, eight broken ribs, three broken vertebrae, a punctured lung, two broken collarbones, bleeding on the brain plus all the superficial wounds.

I went straight into intensive care and all I can remember is BS talking to me. I was in and out of sleep with the amount of medication they were feeding me. It was like a bad dream; every time I opened my eyes I prayed that it was time to go for breakfast at the Tour de France. But it was just more nurses, more tubes, more cables and more pain.

They didn't bother operating on the broken bones; I was told they'd eventually heal themselves. But all I cared about were my legs and whether I'd walk again. Later that night I noticed pins-and-needles in my legs and I started moving my toes which was one of the biggest wins of my life. If I hadn't been in so much pain I would have been doing handstands in the hospital, I was that relieved.

I spent the next week in intensive care, trying to get my head around what had happened. It was pretty scary because every night people would come in screaming—car accident victims and other seriously injured people; it was like living in a bad movie. For the first few days doctors would come in and speak to me, but it was as though they were speaking in a foreign language.

Besides BS, the first person I remember being there was my brother, Darren. Anne-Marie had apparently been there for two days but I don't even remember, which is kind of scary.

Brian and Fay were watching the Tour de France from their lounge room in Adelaide when they noticed something wasn't quite right. 'I said to Fay, "That's funny, I haven't seen Stuey for a while." Just then, Phil Liggett commented that it was one of the most dangerous descents in European racing,' Brian recalls.

'Then soon after he said, "We've just heard that Stuart O'Grady has been injured in a crash." Naturally, I thought, "Oh shit, but he'll be okay, it's only a prang."

'The next thing we heard was, "Stuart O'Grady is being taken by ambulance off the mountain." We saw it on TV but there was absolutely nothing we could do.'

They eventually heard from Anne-Marie, who told them Stuart was alive but badly injured. 'We didn't hear about the extent of his injuries until the next morning but we were just happy he was alive,' Brian says.

Within three days Fay was on a plane to visit Stuart in hospital. 'When I got there he couldn't move. I got a big shock because we'd been able to speak to him on the phone and he'd sounded okay,' Fay says. 'But when he came home we had to dress him and there was a chance he might not get back on the bike again.'

Darren was working for CSC at the Tour de France that year and was at the stage finish with VIP guests when Scott Sunderland told him he had some bad news. 'He took me aside and the world turned inside out for a minute. It was a really bad crash, it was so bad they couldn't tell me how he was,' Darren says.

Anne-Marie was eight months pregnant with their daughter Keira and had just picked up her mother from the airport when she got a text message from her father saying Stuart had been in an accident. 'The next minute I'm trying to arrange to drive five hours to the hospital,' Anne-Marie recalls.

'Unfortunately Stu has had a lot of accidents but that was by far the biggest and the scariest. I've never seen him so vulnerable; it was heartbreaking to see him lying there in hospital. How he gets through such moments and gets back on the bike is beyond me; it takes so much mental strength and dedication,' she says.

Doctors told me that, to the best of their knowledge, when I first crashed I broke my left collarbone and left shoulder blade. Then I flipped onto the other side and broke the other collarbone; then hit the pole and did the eight ribs, the other shoulder blade, three vertebrae and punctured the lung. The ribs were blown to pieces; on the X-rays it looked like somebody had hit me with a sledge-hammer. But by far the worst pain was in my back. Doctors explained that my injuries weren't life-threatening and no internal organs had been damaged; the bones just needed to heal on their own. This was fine; I could deal with it, I could come back.

Having spent a week by my side, Anne-Marie went home. I really wanted to be closer to my family, so I was allowed to be transferred to hospital in Monaco which involved a six-hour drive in the back of the ambulance. This is when I remember getting up for the first time. It was only a few steps to sit in a wheelchair but it was a very big moment for me. I spent another ten days in hospital in Monaco before I was allowed to go home, but it never crossed my mind that I might have ridden my last bike race. No way. I wasn't letting this sport take me out on its terms, especially not lying in a hospital bed. My team manager Kim Andersen came to see me and I remember saying, 'Mate, it's only broken bones, don't worry. Put me down for the Vuelta in September.' Of course I was joking but every time I felt down and out, I started thinking about rehab and my next race. It gave me an objective, and every little progression meant something.

I remember walking down the hallway at home shaking my head because two days earlier I couldn't even get out of bed. They were little steps towards my big goal. People always ask me, 'How do you come back from something like this?' The answer is, it's just a psychological game and a battle to remain positive. The power of the mind can do great things.

I didn't get back on a bike for ten weeks after the accident and the first time was to do twenty minutes on the home-trainer in my sneakers and shorts. I'd lost all my strength, my upper body was depleted and the muscle mass on my legs was gone. It was the longest recovery I've ever had. I was pretty grumpy around the house, in bed I had a bunch of pillows keeping my body at a 45-degree angle to take pressure off my shoulder blades and my ribs were in constant pain. But I had so much support from everyone around me.

Anne-Marie did an incredible job, not only giving birth to our beautiful daughter Keira, but keeping me on the right path with my rehabilitation. She actually gave birth just a few doors down from where I'd been parked in hospital ten days previously, and at one stage I joked that when she went into labour, at least I wouldn't have far to go.

By mid-August I decided that my first race back would be the Herald Sun Tour in Australia in October as part of the national team. It was quite a defining moment for me. On 15 April I won Paris–Roubaix, on 15 July I had my accident, and on 15 October I was pinning on my race number at the Herald Sun Tour. I wasn't there to win; I just wanted to finish the first stage.

On the first day we went up a big climb. Somehow I managed to get over the top with the front group, and as we were plummeting downhill it was blowing a gale. The next thing I knew, a guy right in front of me was blown off the road and crashed into the bushes. I had big carbon 808 Zipp wheels in, which are like disc-wheels that catch the wind, and I thought, 'You have got to be kidding!' I started having flashbacks to July and the Tour de France but I managed to keep it upright. It was a bloody scary introduction back into cycling, I can tell you.

I finished the stage and knew that if I finished one stage, I could finish the Tour. That's where my pre-season started. I was excited like a neo-pro. I can't tell you what it meant to be able to put my leg over a bike and race again because it so easily could have gone the other way. I was a few millimetres away from being in a wheelchair for the rest of my life, or I could have died. But I didn't and I was back.

•

In 2009 we got to Milan–San Remo and, as expected, the first hour was really fast. There are a couple of tricky sections called pave; they're not really cobbles and have nothing on Paris–Roubaix or Tour of Flanders, but they're paves all the same. Guys were saying, 'Be careful, there are cobbles up ahead.' Just as I laughed to myself thinking, 'As if anyone would crash here,' we hit the first section at 60 km/h with a left turn up ahead. Obviously guys just shit themselves when they see these things. I was riding along in cruise control when a group of blokes went sliding across the road. One guy wiped me out and I skidded into a concrete curb which was about 20 centimetres high. My chest bore the full brunt of the impact; I was on all fours and couldn't get my breath. How could guys crash here? Yes, I was hurting but more than anything I was angry.

A couple of people helped me get up. My bike was smashed so I got a new one and the team car towed me back up to the peloton. Bjarne was driving; he got up to 80 km/h and I was hanging on for grim death when I said, 'I've got to let go, this is killing me,' so then he motor-paced me back to the peloton. I tried to get out of my seat to sprint out of a corner but it felt like I was winded; I couldn't get any air in my lungs. A few kilometres later I had to get off my bike because I knew something was broken.

An ambulance took me to hospital. I was waiting for the results of the X-rays when a doctor came in and told me that I hadn't broken anything. I looked at him and said, 'Are you sure? I'm in a fair bit of pain here pal, and I'm not talking crap.' But he told me I'd only done ligament damage and he sent me home. I was in shock but I thought, 'Well, he's the doctor.'

I was parked on the couch at home, cracking open a beer when the phone rang. It was the hospital. 'Mr O'Grady, could you please make your way to the emergency room?' Apparently, another doctor had looked at the X-rays and in actual fact I had a broken collarbone, a couple of broken ribs and I'd a punctured lung. It's the first time in my life I nearly dropped a beer.

Anne-Marie drove me straight back into hospital. Half an hour later, I was lying on a hospital bench with a doctor driving a tube into my chest trying to get air back into my lung. I can't explain the feeling of having a pipe being pushed into your ribcage when you're still awake, but it bloody hurts.

So there I was, two years after the crash that nearly wiped me out, once again propped up with pillows on the couch, ringing a little bell for a glass of water. My old friend pain was back to visit me again.

And there was more to come. I was in Hamburg for the Vattenfall Cyclassics in August 2012—the scene of my 2004 win so I had happy memories of the race. But the real reason I was so motivated was because it was teammate Matt Wilson's last race before his retirement and we were really keen to give him the best possible send-off.

As is the case in some races, it took me 150 km to start feeling good, but we had the whole team up the front and everything was going to plan. It was a hot day and coming through a feed zone was my last opportunity for a water bottle. Normally I wouldn't take one that late in a race— we were going at 60 km/h which is too fast to be grabbing water bottles—but this day it was so warm I changed my mind. We were doing laps of a circuit and earlier I'd noticed water all over the road in a certain section, but it still didn't register with me to be careful.

As we came into the feed zone, there were riders and

soigneurs everywhere. As I reached out to grab the bottle, I realised I was going too fast. Normally the soigneur has a really light grip on it but I was going that fast that our hands kind of gelled together. It was 100 per cent my fault because when our hands came together, my left hand ripped on the brake and my front wheel skidded out from under me right where there was water on the road. There was a big crunch on my shoulder and I banged my head on the ground. I stayed conscious but I was literally seeing stars and I didn't even try to get up. Again, I was looking up at the sky then the crowd was milling around me. I was so pissed off. It's one thing to crash when it's someone else's fault because that just happens, but when you make a mistake, you hate yourself for it. Then I looked over and saw my teammate Jens Keukeleire bleeding everywhere because he'd come down with me. My chain had sliced through his glute muscle like a knife through butter.

I was in so much pain in the back of the ambulance that after continually saying 'Pain, pain!' to the German doctor, he finally whacked an injection into me. I started freaking out. I was in and out of consciousness, then all I could see were trees and it was like I was lying at the bottom of a forest. Weird sounds were going through my head and I was in a really bad place. When the drug finally wore off a good twenty minutes later I said to the doctor, 'What was that?' He told me he'd given me a medication that acts in the same way as LSD. He started apologising for my hallucinations but I cut him off. 'What? Are you joking? You idiot, that's stupid, I thought I was going to die!'

When we got to hospital the doctors came out and told me I'd smashed my collarbone in three places and I'd need surgery. I knew I'd be in hospital for a while so I told the doctors I wanted to go home; I just needed to be closer to my family. But they convinced me to stay overnight. The next day my team masseur came to visit me and I said, 'If they let me out, will you drive me back to Luxembourg?' He looked at me and said, 'Yeah, but do you really want to do that?' I called Andy Schleck who put me on to a specialist surgeon in Luxembourg. I took a handful of the hospital's finest medication, jumped in a car and we hit the road.

I had six-and-a-half hours in the car with pillows banked up around me to make me more comfortable but I felt every single little bump. It was the trip from hell; every breath hurt and every bump was like an electric shock of pain through my body.

We eventually made it to hospital in Luxembourg but when the doctor saw how much skin I was missing he said there was no way he'd be able to operate until it had healed. This meant at least a week in hospital before I could even be operated on.

Everything about it sucked. I'd come off a big year for myself and the team with Orica-GreenEDGE, and even though I didn't win or medal at the London Olympics, it was one of the best days I've ever had on the bike. I was so keen to carry that momentum into the next season, but there I was, back on the couch barely able to move for two weeks at the ripe old age of thirty-nine.

CHAPTER 15

CAPTAIN, MY CAPTAIN

There came a time around 2006 when I had to change my mentality. I still had to think like a winner, but I knew that more often than not, it wouldn't be me up there contesting the victory in the final of a race. I still had one eye on the Classics but I knew that the next phase of my career—and ultimately my longevity in the peloton—would hinge on sacrificing myself for my teammates, and passing on as much experience and knowledge as possible.

It's not an easy transition to make when you've spent almost your entire career trying to cross the finish line first, but I soon realised that I got as much joy out of helping a teammate win as I did from winning myself. For a large part of my career I had a team working for me, and now it was time to do the same for others.

My role started changing in my first year with CSC when Bjarne told me that I could ride the Tour de France but I wouldn't be sprinting for a stage win. Essentially, he was asking me to change my approach from that of a winner to that of a helper—which I accepted and wanted to grasp with both hands. I saw the writing on the wall earlier that year when I was on a training ride in Nice with teammate, Bobby Julich—and I would often think about this afterwards when I was out there suffering on the roads. We were training in the mountains and Bobby looked at me and said, 'Stuey, so you're obviously not going to ride the Tour de France?' I was a bit taken aback and I said, 'Well, I hope I do, I want to.' He said, 'Are you serious? We don't need a sprinter, we're here to win the Tour and if Bjarne selects you, I'll be shocked.' I thought to myself, 'Righty-o, now I'm really going to prove you wrong. I don't just sprint; I can do other things as well.'

I understood I wasn't a mountain climber but who was going to look after the boys in the crosswinds on the flat or medium stages? The Tour de France is not only won in the mountains but in those hectic finishes where you've got to have complete faith in the person in front of you.

I did go to the Tour de France that year, much to Bobby's shock and horror, and rode my arse off doing my job of protecting our leaders. Frank Schleck won the finish on Alpe d'Huez on Stage 15, which was massive, and our team finished with both Frank and Carlos Sastre in the top ten on the final general classification, so it was a successful three weeks.

Everyone knows what the captain of a football team does; they toss the coin or wear the armband, but ultimately decisions that will affect the match are left to the coach on the sidelines. Cycling is different. Road teams have always had captains but these days the role is more defined. It's the guy who not only has the most experience but also the ability to read a race. Reading a race means looking at the weather conditions to work out which way the wind is coming from at the start; you're doing your homework, you don't just rock up and say, 'Today we've got three mountains.' You've got to put a bit of thought into it.

Every night before a big race I would read the race book, look at the direction we're going, then watch the news or get online for a weather report. The wind has a massive influence on a bike race because a headwind or tailwind affects your judgement on how many riders can be in a breakaway. You've also got to know your teammates and which ones are feeling good on race day. So at training or the dinner table, without interrogating the boys, I would ask them, 'How's the form?' Then I'd analyse the team and how we'll approach the race. Can we play poker? Can we bluff the peloton? If everyone knows we've got a top sprinter, other teams will be expecting us to ride on the front. It's like a giant game of chess.

A lot of those decisions are made on the road, which is why we're called road captains. We have directors in the car but they can't feel what's going on in the race, they can't see the guys' faces. But I could, and I could look at anyone in the bunch and see immediately whether they're cruising or whether they're hurting. If that doesn't work—and I could do one of the best poker faces out there when I was hurting—I'd look at the gears they were pushing. Big gears, you know they were tired. One thing Bjarne taught us was to keep our bodies going as well as possible for as long as possible by constantly spinning our legs, eating and drinking. He'd say that time and time again over the radio, so we weren't damaging our muscles and were fresher for the final.

In a cycling team there is a mix of guys. There are those who are ready to sacrifice themselves for the protected rider who will be going for the win, and there are leaders who do a bit of everything and make those key decisions. I guess what made me a good leader was that I'd been in almost every possible situation of a bike race. I'd been a sprinter, a one-day rider for the Classics, won stages of the Tour de France and helped teammates go for the yellow jersey.

I would constantly look ahead and scan the peloton to see where riders were crammed in. Where is Mark Cavendish because that's where the sprinters will be fighting for his wheel and that will be the danger zone for everyone else. That was part of my job and being able to relay that experience to your teammates is all about communication. Even though we're hooked up with radios in our ears, a lot of the time you can't hear anything because of the TV helicopter constantly hovering above or the crowds shouting on the roadside.

Bjarne Riis says Stuart's eagerness to join his team meant a lot to him and he knew Stuart's experience would be a valuable addition as a road captain. 'When you have been a leader you know what it takes,' Riis says. 'We had a guy like Fabian [Cancellara] on the team and I think Stu was very important for Fabian, to guide him, put him in the right position at the right moment. I trust his knowledge and experience in cycling, and to make the right decision at the right time in a race.

'I could definitely use him as my hand in the peloton. I could tell him exactly what I needed and wanted from him and make sure it was done. It was like having a rolling sports director out there.'

Riis says although the pair parted company on disappointing terms, they remain friends. 'Maybe we separated in the wrong way but he knows maybe it was a mistake. I did what I had to do … The worst thing you can do is never [get] over it, but you have to move on and there is a reason for everything.'

In the final years of my career, it would have been a lot easier to sit back and let someone else make those calls; I could have easily done without that stress and responsibility and just rocked up and enjoyed myself. But I knew I wasn't there to win anymore and that's why I was so keen to contribute in any way I could.

Sitting at the dinner table when Andy and Frank Schleck held the yellow jersey during separate Tours de France was amazing, and being there when Carlos Sastre rode onto the Champs Elysées in yellow in 2008—I felt like I'd won the Tour myself. When Fabian won Milan–San Remo in 2008 I was two minutes behind him, and when it came over the radio that he'd won, I was punching the air and screaming, I was that happy.

I began relishing my new role and loved the responsibility and leadership that came with trying to plot a way for our team to win the Tour de France. My 2007 Tour was obviously ruined by the crash, but I'll always treasure the events of 2008.

In the lead-up to the Tour the team had training camps together. We did mountain reconnaissance and went to all the lead-in races together. A few days before the Tour de France started, Bjarne took me aside and said he wanted me to room with Carlos for the next three weeks. 'I want you guys to get to know each other, I want you to have an understanding of each other so when you're on the bike you can trust each other,' he said. Carlos is a pretty quiet guy, he has very much flown under the radar as far as Tour de France winners go, so I knew it would be a real challenge for me. During the last meeting before the Tour, Bjarne turned to me and said, 'Stuey, you're there to protect Carlos, you are to look after him. I don't want to see him in the wind, I don't want to see him wasting one single pedal-stroke of energy.' GC riders can't afford to lose even ten seconds on the bunch sprint days which inevitably mean crazy-dangerous finishes. So Carlos was to sit behind me with absolute confidence that I'd look after him; that there'd be no time gaps between him and his rivals for the yellow jersey.

The race went incredibly well to plan—which in a three-week tour is pretty rare. We had guys like Jens Voigt in the break when it counted, other guys were covering moves when we had to, the Schleck brothers were on good form, Kim Kirchen held the yellow jersey for four days and Frank had it for two days before Carlos made his move on Stage 17 up Alpe d'Huez. That day was the ultimate team victory and showed why cycling is such a team sport. The breakaway had over five minutes on the peloton when we sent Nicki Sorensen to the front to start pacing up the Col du Galibier. Fabian and I drove the bunch approaching the Col de la Croix de Fer and that's when the Schlecks and Kurt-Asle Arvesen took over and sacrificed themselves. When Carlos finally launched up Alpe d'Huez, no one was able to go with him and Frank and Andy marked any threats that were left behind, including Aussie Cadel Evans. Carlos won the stage by 2 minutes 3 seconds from Samuel Sanchez and turned a 49-second deficit into a 1 minute 24 second lead from Frank in the yellow jersey. But the biggest threat was Evans who trailed by 1 minute 34 seconds with four stages, including a 53 km individual time-trial, on Stage 20 to come.

A breakaway posing no threat to the yellow jersey won Stage 18, and Stage 19 was about recovering so Carlos could give absolutely everything in the decisive time-trial before the ride into Paris. Carlos had never been a great time-trialler and 1 minute 34 seconds wasn't a lot of time up his sleeve over a guy like Cadel; to be honest my money was on my countryman catching him.

Carlos and I didn't talk much about the time-trial in our room the night before. He is generally super-relaxed, so I was just an open ear in case he was feeling the pressure. The media frenzy was insane and you can't really prepare for journalists filling your head with insecurities by asking, 'What if, what if?' So I just told him, 'Geez, you're going well mate, you're pedalling well, you look unbelievable on the bike.'

The following day Carlos was amazing. He rode above himself and it had to be the maillot jaune sitting on his shoulders. Wearing the yellow jersey gives you that 10 per cent extra to go deeper into the hurt box. Cadel only gained 29 seconds on Carlos who rode the time-trial of his life, and we protected him all the way into Paris.

I was incredibly honoured when the boys said they wanted me to lead them onto the Champs Elysées. There were guys who had been in the team a lot longer than I had. Kurt-Asle Arversen and I had shared the road captaincy all year, and for him and the other boys to say that they wanted me on the front because of my influence on the team meant a hell of a lot.

It was an incredible Tour de France for CSC-Saxo Bank. Carlos won the yellow jersey, we won the teams classification and a fresh-faced 23-year-old Luxembourger named

Andy Schleck won the white jersey as the Tour's best young rider.

I was at a race in Germany in 2005 when Andy completed his very first race with the professionals; it was like looking at a fifteen-year-old kid. I joked around with him that I'd look after him. Little did I know back then that one day we'd be teammates and the best of friends. I was really intrigued by him and his brother Frank. They were incredibly talented but it was as though they didn't quite know what they were capable of.

After the 2008 Tour de France, Andy came into our room to sign our jerseys and he thanked us for our help. I looked at him and said, 'Mate, you know that you can win this and I'm going to make it my ambition in life to help you win the Tour de France.' It eventually came true in a roundabout way after Andy was awarded the 2010 Tour de France crown retroactively after Alberto Contador went positive. When the decision was handed down, Andy and I weren't even on the same team because I had joined Orica-GreenEDGE but he came to my house and told me he remembered our conversation of four years earlier. He said, 'Even though I've won it in different circumstances, you have helped me achieve my dream.'

Despite achieving so much in my cycling career, I knew I could never win the Tour de France, so helping guys like Carlos and the Schlecks was as good as it gets.

Andy Schleck's earliest memory of Stuart was being invited to celebrate the Australian's birthday after his debut race in Germany. Since then, the two have become close friends. When they were not racing they were regular training partners in Schleck's native country, Luxembourg. 'I don't know what it is, but somehow we've got the right connection,' Andy says.

It was Stuart's loyalty on the bike that won him over. 'He's one of the most committed guys I know. He would die for his teammates on the road. I don't know anyone else who went that deep and pulled for so long for his teammates that he almost couldn't finish the stage himself; that's what makes him so special, and it's why so many guys like him and look up to him.'

Frank Schleck remembers meeting Stuart on a military-style pre-season training camp when they were at CSC. 'He wasn't necessarily the strongest guy at the boot camp who knew how to build a bridge or make a fire, but he was very good at coordinating,' Frank recalls. 'He would say, "Okay, you do this, you take care of this, watch out for this," and he was one of the guys everyone listened to.

'He'd take all the skills of boot camp to a race. He wasn't necessarily the guy who was going to win or the guy going for the GC, but he kept the whole team together and everybody had respect.'

Frank says Stuart's leadership shone through in his decision-making. 'He knew when to make a decision. At times he took the right decision and sometimes he was wrong, but a lot of people never learn how to do that. They don't want to make decisions because they're scared to be wrong. But he made the decision, he took responsibility and we stuck to that plan, right or wrong.'

Fabian Cancellara says Stuart had a calculated plan for every race they started during their time as teammates. 'He came to CSC to be a captain or a leader and he was such an awesome person,' Cancellara says. 'He could see the race, feel the race, talk about the race and change the race. We went to every race with an ideal scenario and you could trust him. For many things he had solutions—somehow it was like he had keys in his pocket.'

It was a role Stuart would continue for the rest of his career, and never was it more important than in the first season for Australian team Orica-GreenEDGE on cycling's WorldTour in 2012.

'We reminded him of his age every now and then but on the bike he's the eyes, ears and the brains of a lot of big races we do,' Australian sprinter Matt Goss says. 'And it takes a lot of pressure off everyone else's shoulders. He definitely makes our life a lot easier by knowing how to deal with different situations because he's been there and done it.'

Goss credits Stuart with helping him land his first ProTour contract with CSC in 2007 after he beat his older compatriot in a criterium a year earlier. He says Stuart has been a mentor to him ever since. 'As a twenty-year-old, I needed somebody to look up to and hang around and Stuey's a good guy for that. Maybe he's the reason I turned into the kind of rider I am—more a sprint and undulating race rider, similar to him,' Goss says.

Even when they were on separate teams in 2011, Goss says Stuart still looked out for him and, in a small way, he helped him become the first Australian to win Milan–San Remo.

'I was coming into the corner of a descent going way too fast and screamed out for him not to turn. I saw him glance back; he could have ended my race right there. I would have t-boned straight into him and we both would have been dragging our arses off the tarmac. But he let me through the gap and didn't put me on the asphalt. When we came across the line, even though we were on different teams, he was one of the first people to shake my hand and congratulate me. I thanked him for not dropping me on that descent.'

I couldn't really say I'm closer with either of the Schleck brothers but I've spent more time with Andy due to our race programs matching up. They're very different guys. Frank is the thinker, he analyses everything and takes things personally whereas Andy is much more blasé and naturally gifted; he doesn't get stressed. He's like a kid in a candy shop, he wants to ride his bike and have fun and that's why it was so much fun conjuring up a plan to win that epic stage on top of the Col du Galibier in 2011.

I had looked at the race book before the Tour and identified its defining stages. Some days the mountains were too far from the finish line which meant a long descent would allow the chasing group to bridge the gap. But Stage 18 was 200.5 km from Pinerolo to Galibier Serre-Chevalier and finished on top of a Category 1 climb—the perfect opportunity for Andy to make up some time on his rivals. He trailed Cadel Evans by 1 minute 18 seconds and Cadel was hanging with him on the climbs. We all knew Cadel was a better time-trialler, so if Andy was to win this race, we had to make it happen.

We were sitting at the back of the bus a few days before when I suggested he make a full-gas attack early when no one was expecting it. We'd try to put a couple of riders in the break and Andy would attack the bunch up an earlier climb and ride across to the leaders, then hopefully keep going all the way to the finish.

I knew it was a pretty out-there plan and that it'd be amazing if it came off, but we had to do something. Usually on a mountainous stage, we'll try to put a rider in the break while the rest of us would get on the front of the peloton to monitor the big-hitters on the first climb, then slowly accelerate up the second climb to put more pressure on. This usually eliminates a lot of guys in the field. You get control of the peloton and then you wind it up faster and faster before leaving it to your leader to launch on the final climb to the finish. But this day we decided our big attack would come on the second climb, the Col d'Izoard, which caught a lot of guys off-guard.

Jens Voigt recalls the moment Stuart gathered the team together in the bus a few days before Stage 18 and proposed his outrageous plan.

'Andy had lost some time on a 5 km rainy descent which put him two minutes back,' Voigt says. 'So Stuey said, "Okay, here's the plan. We hide and recover and in three days we put two riders in the break, we all go flat fuck into the early climb, Andy jumps, catches the two guys in the front and we go."

'Two days before the stage the team started saying, "Oh, I don't know, that's a hard plan, maybe we should watch what the others do?"

'Stuey said, "Look, I've had enough of this, this is the plan, we go balls to the wall and take it all in glory or we go down fighting."

'That's what he's good for and people listen to him. When he does make a serious face, people actually listen to him.'

Andy says he initially hesitated about the plan but trusted Stuart's judgement. 'In the beginning maybe it was a stupid plan but in the end it worked out. And Stuey was the last man standing for me that day, it was a perfect day.'

I reckon because I helped hatch the plan, I climbed as well as I have in my life that day. I was the last rider left on the team in front of Andy when he attacked, which was unheard of. I was on a mission, I was anxious for the plan to come off and I wanted to see what damage Andy could do. Eventually, only Jens was in front of me and Andy behind me; then finally just the two of us. I launched him into his attack and he went on to win one of the greatest stages in Tour de France history.

It was awesome to see my battle plan come off. Afterwards some people questioned why Andy would go so deep that day; they reckoned he should have just hung in there and tried to do a better time-trial. But in reality, he was always going to be beaten in a time-trial, so it was a fantastic outcome.

Cadel rode his way to the yellow jersey in the time-trial, which was an incredible moment. I've watched Cadel's entire career and he's always been a really intriguing character. Mountain-bikers tend to have a different personality because it's all about themselves; I imagine when they come into road cycling it's quite a big change. It probably took him a little while to find his feet in that environment but he's always had a massive engine and is a huge talent. Fifteen years ago I'm sure I would have said if any Australian rider was going to win the Tour de France it would be

Cadel. By the time he did win the Tour in 2011, everyone had almost forgotten about his near win in the Giro d'Italia in 2002 when he was fourteenth and wore the pink jersey, so it should have been no surprise. He always had the potential to win the Tour; he just needed the right team.

Despite both of us being road cyclists, it took a few years before Cadel and I crossed paths; we were on different teams and following different race programs. But when we did eventually meet, we got along fine and always have.

I was team leader the day he won the world championship in 2009. The beauty of the Australian team is that unlike some countries, once you're selected for the national team, you leave any competition or rivalry at the door. Everyone's on the same page. I had to make some big calls the day Cadel won the rainbow jersey, and when he crossed the line first we were jumping around the bus like crazy because we realised we'd just witnessed a historical moment. Similarly, when Cadel won the Tour de France in 2011, I was one of the happiest guys in the peloton. During the race the media kept asking me, 'What's it like trying to hinder an Australian from winning the Tour de France?' I hated this question because of course I wanted to see an Australian win the yellow jersey, but I'm a professional bike-rider and had a job to do for my own leaders, the Schleck brothers. When we got to Paris on 24 July, I was one of the first people to congratulate him.

My decision to join the Schlecks' team at Leopard a year earlier was incredibly difficult. Without doubt, CSC-Saxo Bank had been the best team I'd ever been a part of. Bjarne is not perfect, but who is? He got the best out of every bike-rider who came through his team so leaving was hard, but the end came quite quickly given what happened during the 2010 Vuelta à España. When Fabian saw me leave he got itchy feet and wanted to join the party as well, so I felt for Bjarne because he'd had something special but it was gone in an instant. Leopard was the Schlecks' own Lux-embourg team, and one of the main reasons I joined was because I still believed I could help them win the Tour de France.

I only had one season with Leopard, but we experienced some incredible highs—such as Andy's stage win at the Tour—but also one of the darkest times of not just our cycling careers, but our lives.

I didn't know Wouter Weylandt very well until we became teammates in 2011 but we quickly became friends because he was a really likable guy. He fitted in perfectly with the team—even though he was the only Belgian bloke I knew who didn't like beer. We did the Belgian Classics in spring and afterwards I told him I was taking my family to Dubai for a holiday. Wouter had only recently found out he would be riding the Giro d'Italia, but he said, 'Stuey, do you reckon I could sneak over to Dubai for a few days with my wife and have a holiday?' He was really worried the team would find out he was taking a break before the Giro but I told him, 'Yeah, why not? Go and re-charge the batteries, I won't tell anyone, just go and enjoy some time with your wife.' I ran into them when we were in Dubai and we were meant to catch up for a drink but for some reason it didn't happen so I just sent him a text message wishing him luck for the Giro. That was the last time I spoke to him.

9 May 2011 is a day I will never forget. I had just got home from training when I went online and read that Wouter had been killed in a crash on the descent of the Passo del Bocco during Stage 3 of the Giro. I was absolutely devastated and broke down in tears. Not only had we lost a teammate and a friend, but I knew Wouter had a pregnant wife at home. Cycling is a dangerous job and Wouter's passing really hit home because I'd been so close on so many occasions. I'd be lying if I said I didn't fear the worst while I was racing. Even when I was out training, my life was in other people's hands and there were so many close shaves and near misses. So to see someone leave the world doing what they love was bloody scary.

It really knocked everyone on the team, but it never entered my mind to give cycling away. I suppose deep down I also knew that Wouter wouldn't have wanted me to make such a decision. But coming home that day I hugged my kids a bit longer and told them I loved them. Such moments pull you closer, and remind you never to take anything for granted. I remember suffering in a bike race not long after Wouter's death and saying to myself, 'This isn't suffering.' A death puts everything into perspective and I still thought about him whenever I was on a bad day.

CHAPTER 16

FOR MY COUNTRY

There had been so many whispers and rumours about attempts to set up an Australian team in the past that I was beginning to think it almost certainly wouldn't happen in my time on the bike. But when Australian businessman, long-time cycling supporter and friend Gerry Ryan called me at home in Monaco two days after the 2011 Tour de France, I knew he was serious.

Just twelve months earlier in 2010 I had been part of quite a serious bid to build Australia's first professional team. I'd been approached by a group of people with a strong business plan who were talking to a major international company. My job was to pick a hypothetical roster, should it go ahead. But at the end of the day you've got to have the money in the bank, and in this instance, the sponsor didn't come through so it was back to the drawing board. I had made (longtime cycling coach and administrator) Shayne Bannan aware of it, and I think that got the wheels turning in his mind, and was probably what ignited the fire in Gerry to make it happen a year later.

Shayne eventually approached me in early 2011 to say there was something on the horizon. While he understood that I was committed to Leopard, he wanted to give me plenty of notice. It was a tricky situation because I was in the best team in the world in terms of rankings. We were winning big races and I was super-happy. But the option of an Australian team was constantly in the back of my mind, and when my phone rang on the Tuesday after the 2011 Tour de France and a voice said, 'Hi Stuey, it's Gerry Ryan,' everything suddenly became very real.

I've known Gerry for more than twenty years and the relationship has grown stronger over time. One of my earliest memories of meeting him was when he invited Anne-Marie and me to Flemington to watch the Melbourne Cup in the early 2000s. He came up to me early in the day and said, 'Stuart, I've heard you've got this junior development team in Adelaide,'—which I did, designed to act as a feeder team to the South Australian Sports Institute so kids who started cycling wouldn't get sidetracked by footy, soccer or cricket. Gerry said, 'I'd like to give you some money for this.' When I told him what our major sponsor was putting in, he said, 'Well, I'd like to match that.' I was blown away. It involved quite a substantial amount of money, we weren't talking about a few grand here or there. I still couldn't believe it, so later in the day I went up to him and said, 'Are you serious?' Gerry looked me straight in the eye and said, 'Stuey, I told you I'll give you the money. I'm giving you the money.'

So when he rang me in July 2011 to tell me he was going to fund what he hoped would be Australia's first World-Tour cycling team, I knew it was on. This wasn't a rumour anymore; it was Gerry Ryan. He said he wanted me to know that he'd love to have me on board but there was absolutely zero pressure because he understood my current situation. I told him I really appreciated the call but that I was happy at Leopard and would probably stay there because although I hadn't re-signed, I had spoken with the team owner at the time-trial of the Tour de France and we'd organised a meeting to get the deal done.

But after that call from Gerry, Shayne rang me a couple more times and I kept toying with the idea. I just couldn't get past the thought of an Australian team in the World-Tour and not being part of it. My biggest fear was picturing the teams' presentation at the start of the Tour Down Under in Adelaide where 'Australia's first ProTour team' would be announced—without me.

The thing that eventually clinched my decision was Matt White. Whitey had been appointed a director with the team and said he really wanted my experience for these young Australian guys they were taking on. The more I thought about my future and where I wanted to head, the more I thought about that day with Gerry at the Melbourne Cup and how much he'd given to the sport. Gerry has been an enormous support for me through the good times and the bad, and without him cycling would be nowhere near as successful and popular in Australia as it is today. Furthermore, I'd known Shayne since I was sixteen and Whitey was one of my best friends. Yes, it was a risk because it was a step into the unknown, but it would have felt so wrong if I wasn't there. In August I'd moved my family from Monaco to Luxembourg where we bought a home, partly because I imagined I'd be riding for Leopard for the rest of my career, then become a sporting director or manager with the Schlecks' team. So the last thing anyone expected when I moved to Luxembourg was that I would leave the team within a week of arriving. We were still unpacking boxes at home when Shayne rang and said, 'Sorry to push you here, but I need a decision by 2 pm on Saturday.'

Shayne Bannan says he knew he had to sign Stuart but was conscious of putting him under too much pressure.

'There's a lot of history between Stuart and Australian cycling. He's one of the icons of the sport and because he's such a great leader, he was right up there in the first three or four riders we needed to have on the team [Orica-GreenEDGE]. He's been involved in GC winning teams, green jerseys, team pursuit world championships; across the spectrum of cycling he is arguably one of the most experienced guys the sport has seen … if I think of one word to describe him, it's tenacity. Under any circumstances or conditions, he just comes out with that same never-say-die attitude.'

Gerry Ryan remembers watching Stuart compete in the 1992 Barcelona Olympics, and over the years they became close friends. Ryan says he knew of Stuart's reputation as a tough man on the bike but saw it for himself at the Tour of Ireland in the mid-2000s. 'It was pissing rain and windy when he went out the front. The other riders were saying it was the worst day they had ridden in. But the boy—he didn't let it worry him,' Ryan recalls.

'I had the Jayco-AIS team there—juniors like Jack Bobridge and Cam Meyer who looked up to him. Stuey's toughness that day will always stay in my memory.

'We saw it as a priority to get him for GreenEDGE; we needed someone with his leadership qualities and mental toughness to mentor the younger blokes. As an individual he's approachable and very humble ... that's what I've always liked about him— his humility. He takes cycling seriously but himself not.'

It was 6 August—mine and daughter Keira's birth-day—so we had the Schleck brothers and their parents over for a barbecue to celebrate. Little did they know, but that morning I'd decided to take the plunge and go with GreenEDGE. I told Anne-Marie but I needed to tell the boys before I made the phone call to Shayne because out of loyalty to them, I felt they should know first.

The Schlecks arrived for the barbecue. I gave them a beer and asked them to come upstairs, then told them I was going to leave the team. Their jaws nearly dropped out of their heads but when I explained there was a start-up Australian team that I really wanted to be part of, their response was the opposite to what I'd been expecting. 'That's awesome,' they said. They'd just been through a similar thing by starting their own Luxembourg team so they could appreciate the opportunity I'd been given. They each gave me a big hug and a handshake and it meant so much to see how happy they were for me.

Telling the Schlecks was hard, but not as hard as telling Fabian. As teammates at CSC and Leopard, we were so close that during some of his negotiations with the bosses of the biggest teams in the world, he'd put them on speakerphone so I could listen in. Some of the money that was being thrown at him—if I hadn't heard it myself I wouldn't have believed it. But Fabian would say, 'No, I want to stay here with the boys, we're such a special group.' They'd say, 'Fabian, you name your price,' but he'd reply, 'It's not about the money, it's this group we have.'

When I told him I was leaving he was pretty pissed off initially, until I could explain it properly. He then realised that I had a twenty-year relationship with Gerry Ryan, and he understood that I simply had to be part of such a significant Australian project.

As reality dawned that we had a serious team in the

making, the names kept coming on board. We had Gerro (Simon Gerrans) and Gossy (Matt Goss), Cookie (Baden Cooke), Durbo (Luke Durbridge), Heppy (Michael Hepburn) and Howard (Leigh Howard). With each guy jumping in, it became more and more exciting.

Our first national championship in Ballarat in January 2012 was nerve-racking because we knew that if we lost that race with seventeen riders on the start line, questions would be asked. But we were racing guys who were coming off the national road series and this was their world championship so they had good form. Thankfully Gerro came through with the goods that day with a thrilling sprint finish. It was like we'd won the Tour de France.

We went to the Tour Down Under where Gerro continued his great form, and that whole week was a dream come true. It was one of the proudest moments of my career.

We never looked back in our first year. Internally things went as smoothly as they appeared to from the outside. We refused to use 'It's our first year' as an excuse for any race we started. We had a few meetings in our training camps in November where we agreed that just because we had a first-year set-up, we weren't neo-pros and didn't need to ride like neo-pros. Durbo was winning races, Gossy won a stage of the Giro, we won the team time-trial at Tirreno-Adriatico and Gerro won Milan–San Remo—the oldest and longest race in Europe.

I'm not sure the average person can appreciate the magnitude of that result. Before the race I told Gerro everything I knew about Fabian, who was one of the big favourites. I tried to explain where he was going to attack and what to do—or what not to do when Fabian decided to drill it all the way to the finish. Like everyone on our team, Gerro rode the perfect race. When he won, it was a massive, massive moment.

The only box we didn't tick in our first year was a stage win at the Tour de France. Nevertheless, it was surreal just to be standing on stage for the teams' presentation before the start. I looked down at Gerry and Shayne, and if they didn't have a tear in their eye they must have had some bad hayfever. The highlight of my 2012 season was in London during my sixth and final Olympic Games. Once again, just being selected was a mission because we could have sent two teams to London. It really showed how far Australian cycling had come. These days, none of us goes to the Olympics to get a bag of goodies and a free green-and-gold tracksuit. We no longer have the mentality of twenty years ago when we'd be happy if an Australian simply finished the road race. Rather, we went to London expecting to win, and I knew that having to do nine laps of the undulating course around Surrey for 250 km was going to be brutal. I also knew that with teams of only five riders, it would be physically impossible for one nation—mainly Great Britain looking after the red-hot favourite Mark Cavendish—to control a bunch of 140 bike-riders.

I came out of the Tour de France feeling strong. Without race radios in London the team would need someone to make the calls out there on the roads. We had a fantastic team that included Cadel Evans, Mick Rogers, Gossy and Gerrans. Some of the guys were a little bit sick, which we kept quiet from the media, but it meant my role would be even more important on race day. We had a lot of meetings leading up to the road race, which was where my strength really came out. I told the boys that we'd all won big races in our careers, and how did we do that? By being aggressive, by attacking and leading from the front, which was what we'd need to do to get a result at the Olympics.

The night before, Whitey gave me the job of being in the first breakaway of the day. To be honest, I had mixed feelings about his decision. I'd be lying if I said I wasn't dreaming of winning an Olympic gold medal on the road, even at my age, so my response in my head was, 'Oh man, that's my day done. I won't be there in the final.' But I also understood that my role now was to ride for the team, and I was prepared to sacrifice myself for the boys. We decided the perfect scenario would be for me to get in a breakaway and try to make the lead as big as possible; then Mick Rogers or Simon Gerrans would be in the next wave that came across; and the third and final wave would rely on Cadel attacking or Gossy winning a sprint if it came to that.

The break got away inside the first 30 km and the noise from the crowds was deafening. I'd never experienced anything like it in my life; it was so loud you couldn't even talk to the rider next to you. It was the complete opposite to the Beijing Olympics in 2008 where it was eerily quiet because the roads had been closed to spectators and the only people on the course were military guys at every 200 metres. There were so many people in London you couldn't even see where the corners were, so we were flying around blind.

Just as I put the hammer down I saw a dog run across the road behind me. I knew the dog would cause mayhem in the peloton, so cunningly I decided this was the chance to break away. I really pushed it hard the first couple of kilometres and turned around to see eleven others with me; I was literally screaming at them to keep going. We had some serious horsepower in the break with guys like Denis Menchov, Michael Schar, Marco Pinotti and Jurgen Roelandts driving us along.

After a while I dropped back to the commissaire's car and learned that we had three-and-a-half minutes on the peloton, so I rode back up to the break and said, 'Boys, let's get it to six minutes,' which meant we could afford to lose one minute per lap. I remember Swiss rider Schar telling me, 'But Fabian is behind us.' I said, 'Yeah, and this is perfect, just go mate'—and off we went. I did quite a lot of work but on every climb, I sat dead last. I wanted to save every single ounce of energy because I had a good feeling about our breakaway. Every time I looked at my green and gold jersey and shorts, I was reminded that this was the last time I would ride for Australia at the Olympics and it lifted me.

When we still had a five-minute lead with four-and-a-half laps to go, I began to think we might be a chance to hang on. We lost time up the climb but I knew we would gain it on the downhill when the peloton would be ultra-cautious.

I'm sure Great Britain thought they had the break under control but I knew it would be impossible for Cavendish to get over that climb nine times and be in a winning position. Eventually a group was going to come across to us but when I heard it was teammate Mick Rogers who was in no-man's land on a solo attack, I was a little disappointed because I knew he wouldn't bridge it on his own. But at the same time it meant I didn't have to do a turn in the breakaway because when the boys said, 'Work, work,' I could say that I had Mick Rogers coming across—so I had two laps to sit in and recover, which would prove crucial later on.

Mick eventually got swallowed up by the bunch and soon after, by the roar from the crowd I knew there was a fair dinkum attack going on behind us. I was praying for a green and gold jersey to ride up alongside my wheel, but to my horror, there was none. Because we were racing without radios, we had people standing along the course holding signs with colours and letters to form secret signals. A green board meant 'good situation'; red meant 'bad situation'; and a time board with dots showed the number of riders in the breakaway, how many riders were chasing and the time gap. For the duration of my time in the breakaway, we had a massive green sheet which was perfect. But when we were caught, bang, it went red, and to make it worse, there were no little yellow dots to tell me an Australian rider was coming across to us. All of a sudden our perfect plan went to shit and I thought, 'I'm going to have to salvage a result for my country here. A medal would be pulling a rabbit out of a hat but I've got to get a top ten.'

In the break there were four Swiss riders, including Fabian; four Spaniards; and four Italians who were among the best in the world—but none of our boys. The situation turned critical. In my opinion Fabian would have won that day had he not crashed, so I parked on his wheel and asked him to let me know when he was going to attack. On every pedal-stroke I was on the verge of cramping and there were a few little attacks but the turning point was Fabian's crash. When he went down coming out of a corner, suddenly the favourite was gone.

After the initial shock, everyone quickly realised that the gold medal was up for grabs so I sat behind Philippe Gilbert with 1 km to go but when he attacked he swung around, saw I was on his wheel and pulled over which cost me a lot of energy and was another bullet out of my barrel. The big wave came past and I elbowed as best I could, giving it everything. Every muscle fibre in my body was burning, my earlobes felt like they were full of lactic acid and I was in a blur of pain and noise. I had a quick look up, saw the finish less than 200 metres away and gave it everything. It wasn't enough to win, but I managed to grab sixth place behind Alexander Vinokourov who took the gold medal. I then collapsed on the side of the road. I had never been so empty in my life, not even after winning Paris–Roubaix was I that drained. I realised that sixth wasn't what we were after but I could not have ridden any better that day. I was proud that it was a top-ten for Australia, and given the situation we'd found ourselves in, it saved the day. Anne-Marie and the kids were there with their faces painted in the

Aussie colours and everyone in Australia was watching on TV. It's those days that I lived for; they made the years of suffering worthwhile.

It had been a massive season for me and Orica-GreenEDGE. The Olympic road race was my final big goal as I wouldn't be riding the world championships. I just had to get through the Vattenfall Cyclassics, then I could look forward to the off-season for a welcome break and not think about cycling for a while.

But the exact opposite happened. On 19 August I crashed in Hamburg and smashed my collarbone. Then a week later the biggest storm to ever hit cycling began to break. It started on 25 August when Lance Armstrong announced he would no longer fight US Anti-Doping Agency charges that threatened to strip him of his seven Tour de France titles.

I didn't read the whole Reasoned Decision document but gathered what I could from what was being reported online and it shocked me because it was incredible to read the lengths some guys went to. I was aware of what I had done, obviously, and had done my best to bury it, but this came as a shock. I used to idolise Lance and I guess I got caught up in the fairytale story. I heard him speak, he was inspiring and that's what captivated the world. Lance was more than just a cyclist. He had the aura of a Michael Jordan or Muhammad Ali, and when someone like that walks into the room you take notice. Was he arrogant? Yes. Did he have an ego the size of Texas? Of course he did. But I've seen a lot of champions and that's what they need to get to that level.

The revelations shocked me but above all they scared me. Despite all the rumours and accusations of doping, I honestly didn't think Lance would ever come down. I thought he was too big and too powerful so for him to be brought down was huge; it showed that no one is safe if you've done the wrong thing.

Within days of the USADA report being released there was another bombshell—this time, closer to home. Whitey admitted to doping during his career. By this stage nothing really shocked me anymore and I told the media that Whitey was a pawn in a bad chess game. He was used and abused and felt like he had no choice when the pressure became too much. We are all human and people make mistakes—the level of mistake needs to be taken into consideration—but people like Whitey made a bad decision. Since then, all he has ever done on and off the bike is sacrifice himself for other people. When he came on board as a director sportif it was his life, his passion, and he was involved with Garmin and their anti-doping policies for years. He admitted he had a muddy past but he used it to make sure that other riders never went down that avenue.

Weeks after the USADA bombshell I did an interview in which I said doping had never been an option for me. I knew it wasn't the truth but what was my alternative? Admit what I had done and be burned at the stake? I began to realise that something was probably going to come out at some stage but deep down I was hoping it wouldn't. I was being selfish, I wanted to protect myself, my family and every-thing I had achieved after the 1998 Tour de France—all of which was legitimate. I didn't want my whole career to be tarnished over a couple of weeks of bad decisions.

By January 2013, I was back in Adelaide for the Tour Down Under. A few days before the race was due to start, Lance confessed in a live TV interview. Straight after I fronted a room full of journalists and it was really hard answering questions about him, knowing that I had experimented with EPO earlier in my career. One journalist asked me whether I'd ever have a beer with Lance again and I said I wouldn't. That was a gut-wrenching experience, but I was looked upon as one of the elder statesmen of cycling who'd raced Lance back then, so what was I meant to say? I was lying, but in my head what I'd done all those years ago wasn't even in the same ballpark as this whole affair.

There will always be those who say, 'You cheat once, you cheat forever' but I don't agree with that at all. I think people make mistakes and have the right to come back and prove otherwise. It's like smoking a joint at school: does that make you a drug user for life? I don't think so. But by January 2013, perspective on our sport and trust in cycling had gone out the window.

A lot of people have asked me why I didn't confess right then and there, but when you've been keeping something inside you for fifteen years you're not just going to blurt it out; the consequences would have been huge. So I just went into autopilot and denied ever having used drugs.

I gave the same answers during interviews I did as part of anti-doping investigations, including the team's Nicki Vance review. Again, that was really hard. I was talking with

Nicki, for whom I had the utmost respect because of her work with ASADA and because she understands the differences in the sport between then and now. But I was in a very difficult situation. It was right in the middle of the Tour Down Under, we'd just seen the biggest bust in cycling history and did I want to blurt out that I'd had a dabble in 1998? I'd seen what had happened to Whitey and I didn't want to bring the team or myself down. I couldn't bring myself to do it and there's no one else to blame for that but myself.

By 2013, cycling had changed so much and all for the better. There will always be cynics but hopefully those people look at the sport and see how much is being done, not just at racing but behind the scenes, to fight doping. Cycling is the most tested sport on the planet; there is a whereabouts system whereby riders have to state exactly where they will be for certain hours of the day, every day of the year. There is also a biological passport so blood parameters are in a data bank and monitored for any abnormalities. As I would learn, if you cheat, no matter how long ago, you will be caught and the net is only getting tighter.

CHAPTER 17

COMING CLEAN

In February 2013, I left Anne-Marie and the kids at home in Luxembourg and flew to Girona in Spain for a week-long personal training camp. It had been one of the coldest and longest European winters on record—our pool had turned into an ice-skating rink and Anne-Marie had been shovelling snow out of the driveway just to get the kids to school every morning while I was away racing. As a Classics rider it was crucial that I be doing long, hard kilometres on the road in preparation. An hour on the indoor trainer at home wasn't going to cut it so training in Luxembourg wasn't an option. I got on the internet and booked a flight to Spain where I knew the weather would at least allow me to get outside. Saying goodbye to Anne-Marie and the kids was horrible. I had only spent two days with them all year and this was a self-imposed trip away. But Anne-Marie was as understanding as ever and insisted I do what was best for me.

The weather wasn't too bad in Girona but on the final morning I pulled back the curtains to see a freezing cold and wet morning for my last training ride before heading home. I called around to see if any of my mates were up for a ride but they had either decided to do something else or hold out to see if the weather improved. I had no such option; I was there to train so I bought a map of the area and rode off on my own. Henk Vogels and I once lived not far from Girona in a place called L'Estartit so I decided it would be a good opportunity to visit my former home town.

It was pissing down rain and blowing a gale when I left Girona all kitted up to retrace my training roads from seventeen years ago. As I rode along a pretty boring stretch of road, I started thinking about what had brought me here all those years ago, and how funny it was that two decades later I was still banging my head against the same brick wall headwind that you never seemed to escape down there. I began to see the signs to L'Estartit and I couldn't resist. I pulled out my phone, took a photo welcoming me to the small coastal village and sent it to Henk who was back in Australia probably about to go to bed.

As I took off again I started having flashbacks of the same dodgy little shops and villas perched up on the hillside. Our supermarket was still standing but only in a skeleton form of broken bricks crumbling from the timber frame.

Hunting for a cafe to warm up, out of the corner of my eye I spotted a sign that read David's Bike Shop. What the hell? Surely not. This couldn't be the same bike shop, and even if it was, it couldn't be the same bloke running it. I pedalled over, and sure enough it was the same place where we used to hang out after training, where we bought our spare tyre tubes and talked with David, the owner. His son had taken us motor-pacing a couple of times and they'd even invited us to their family home for Sunday dinner all those years ago. I had to go in and see if he was still there.

As I opened the door, an old man appeared from out the back where he had been quietly repairing an old mountain bike. The look on his face was priceless. Without any hesitation I asked, 'David?' 'Stuart!' he yelled as a huge smile spread across his face. I could not believe it. It had been seventeen years since I'd been in that bike shop. Back then I was a 23-year-old kid with a dream of making a cycling career in Europe. Now I walked in as a Paris–Roubaix champion and an Olympic gold medallist; I'd ridden sixteen Tours de France, won stages and worn the yellow jersey; and I was a proud husband and father of three beautiful kids.

As we stood around chatting, David told me that the internet was killing his bike shop business and that no one was coming in to buy things anymore. Feeling guilty, I looked around and decided to buy a spare tyre and whatever else I could find just to help him out. I showed him photos of my three gorgeous kids and wife and said goodbye.

I then found a cafe on the beach, ordered a coffee and a

sandwich and sat there staring out to sea. I really had come full circle. Perhaps I should have stopped riding then and there, but I was committed to the team for at least another year and wasn't ready to retire.

●

In April 2013, I competed in Paris–Roubaix. Dad had come over to watch the race for the first time and I wanted to go all-in and give 100 per cent. We had Sebastian Langeveld as our team leader, who achieved a great result, but I didn't have a great ride, and the only reason I finished was because Dad and my family were in the velodrome waiting for me.

By now I was getting sick of people asking me, 'When are you going to retire?' so I decided to put a date on it and work towards a finish line. After speaking with the team, we decided it would be at the 2014 Tour de France. But I had to get through the 2013 Tour de France first and, looking back now, I honestly don't know how I did it.

The story about the French senate report and French cyclist Laurent Jalabert started bubbling the day before I left Luxembourg to go to the Tour. While having breakfast at the kitchen table at home, I read a story about an investigation into the 1998 race and how retroactive tests on samples from '98 were done in 2004 and would be publicly released to reveal which riders had tested positive to EPO. In that moment, I felt like the ground had opened up and swallowed me whole. I must have looked pale because Anne-Marie asked if I was feeling alright. I read out the story and Anne-Marie said, 'Well, you've got nothing to worry about, you never did anything wrong.' And that was the beginning of the end, mentally anyway. I was about to leave for a record-breaking seventeenth Tour de France, I'd trained and sacrificed so much, but it all went out the window when I read this report about the 1998 Tour. I thought about my successes of that year and what I'd done building up to the Tour, and I just felt so empty.

I went to the start of the Tour in Corsica but I couldn't get the senate report out of my mind. I tried to put on a brave face, be a leader and motivator, but it was ridiculously hard. If anyone noticed something was up, it wasn't mentioned. I didn't try to find out anything further about the report because I didn't want to raise suspicions in case people started wondering why I was bringing it up. So I just shut up and suffered in silence.

It was a blessing when the race started because for a very brief time, it was all that mattered to me. My teammate Simon Gerrans won Stage 3, which was amazing, and the following day we had the chance to put him in the yellow jersey with the team time-trial. By now I was feeling a lot of anger and uncertainty. I wanted to prove that I was here and was 100 per cent—which I did.

To win the team-time trial by one second was beyond amazing, and standing up on stage with the boys, I was overwhelmed by emotion. Behind the presentation I was in tears, knowing that at almost forty years of age I'd managed to contribute to a team effort on such a monumental occasion. For a few minutes I forgot about everything else that was going on. Two days later we had Daryl Impey in the yellow jersey; to have one of the nicest blokes in the peloton leading the race in your own team—well, it made me so happy.

But deep down I knew the writing was on the wall. More stories were emerging that forty riders could be named in the report. I was well aware that in 1998 I had the yellow jersey, stood on the podium and was drug-tested so I accepted that it was only a matter of time before my name came out.

Originally the senate report was supposed to be released after Stage 18 to Alpe d'Huez but for some reason it was postponed. I think this was to protect the Tour de France because of the potential fallout during the current race. Yet I expected it to be tabled then, so that's when I planned to tell the team and Anne-Marie.

It's hard to get one-on-one time with anyone at the Tour de France, let alone when you're one of nine riders on a team. But I knew the Stage 17 individual time-trial from Embrun to Chorges on 17 July was my best hope of sitting down with general manager Shayne Bannan to tell him what was going on. It had been such a magical Tour for the team and I didn't want to wreck things; but at the same time, after everything Shayne had done for me over the years, he had to know.

I actually managed to do a pretty good 32 km time-trial; I must have been riding on emotion and adrenaline because for a while I was leading, but it was very early in the day.

Afterwards I called Shayne to say there was a chance my

name would be on the list of riders in the French senate report. When I met with him later I explained that it was because of what I had done leading into the 1998 Tour de France. I didn't feel relief, just more of that hollow, empty feeling that I had been unable to escape for the previous two weeks.

Bannan says his message to Stuart was to be honest about everything.

'Stuart did inform me on the day of the time-trial that he wasn't too sure what the report would bring regarding him being named or not. The rumours had circulated for a while, but that often seems to be the case during the Tour. I urged him to tell the truth and also reiterated his obligation to keep us informed and face the consequences if something differed from the statements he'd given to the Nicki Vance report and to the different inquiries.

'After the Tour he wanted to announce his retirement straight away and we did so according to his desire. Tuesday he called me and told me that he wanted to admit and talk about this with the media.'

After Stage 18, expecting the senate report to be released, I called Anne-Marie and asked her to come to my hotel at the top of Alpe d'Huez. She came, but Dad happened to go with her for a walk and when they got there, I suddenly felt that it wasn't the right time to break the news. It would have put them in a catastrophic hurt bag and I couldn't bear to see my wife and Dad hit with the news at that moment. So, not knowing what the next few days would hold, I told them, 'Make sure you enjoy the rest of the week and enjoy Sunday in Paris because it's going to be a special occasion.' I didn't elaborate, but I think I hinted strongly enough that it was probably going to be my last race.

As we got closer to Paris, I realised that I really didn't have the drive to continue riding anymore. It was a hard tour and I'd had enough. I knew that winning the teams time-trial two weeks earlier was as good as it would ever get for me again. The final two mountain stages to Le Grand Bornand and Mont Semnoz were about the hardest two days I've ever had to deal with on a bike. They were incredibly difficult physically but mentally I wasn't there, I was on another planet and found it hard to focus. Of course I didn't want my career to end this way but it was happening whether I liked it or not. The report still wasn't out but it may as well have been because I'd already confessed to Shayne. By now I was very reserved and feeling so ashamed of what I'd done. I was imagining what would happen in the media and what the consequences would be. It was like watching a movie that starts off good but ends really badly, and I was the main actor.

I had a lot of family on the Champs Elysées when we

got to Paris—my parents, my mother- and father-in-law, my sister, brother-in-law and my kids; they were all just enjoying the moment. That night we had a quiet dinner and I went back to stay with the team at the hotel. I decided that the following day I would tell my family my secret. The next morning I got a taxi to their apartment, walked in, told them I had something to say and asked them to listen.

I didn't have a pre-meditated speech, there was no way I could make it sound good. I just wanted them to at least try to understand the situation back then and why I had made that bad decision.

For a while, I couldn't get the words out. When I did, it was the worst moment of my life. When I finished speaking, I expected someone to walk up and punch me for being so stupid. But their reaction was the exact opposite. I was expecting the worst but they were very supportive and emotional, there were lots of tears and lots of hugs.

When I spoke to Dad days later, he said at the time he thought I was going to tell them I was sick and dying so his reaction was almost relief. His comment did help me put things into perspective—that people around the world are going through a lot worse than I was, every day. Yes, this was a bad mistake; yes, it was going to hurt me and a lot of people; but I was still healthy and I had my family.

Brian O'Grady says that when Stuart hinted to him and Fay that Stage 21 in Paris would be his last race as a professional and he would retire, he was surprised but didn't ask any questions. 'My conclusion was that he was mentally exhausted and he'd had enough of the lifestyle,' Brian says.

'In Paris on the final day, I had this great feeling of sadness that our son, who had had such a wonderful career and was loved and admired by so many, would end his last ever race with no fanfare at all after such a quick decision to retire.

'The next day we were at the apartments and got a message saying Stuart was coming over and wanted to speak to us before we went out sightseeing––but I was expecting that because that's when he'd explain why he'd suddenly retired. When he got there he asked us to get a drink and take a seat, then he took one of the kitchen chairs and sat it out the front of everyone. I still had no inkling of what he was about to say.

'Then it became really horrible, distraught is the only word I can think of to describe him, because he could barely speak. And for about twenty seconds before the words came out of his mouth was the worst time of my life. I thought he was going to tell us he had a terminal illness and that's why he had to stop riding because I couldn't imagine anything that could make him so distraught.

'When he finally said for two weeks before the 1998 Tour de France he took EPO, I nearly jumped up and said, "For fuck's sake, is that all?" In a way, I was relieved. But of course I couldn't jump up and down because it was still a big admission to a big mistake. He told us he was telling us the truth, the whole truth and nothing but the truth.'

After the Tour, Brian and Fay spent time with Stuart, Anne-Marie and the kids in Luxembourg before returning to Adelaide where Stuart's confession had gone public.

'Fay and I were disappointed with Stuart, but you have got to take things in context,' he says. 'When we got back to Australia we were overwhelmed by the support from people. We were sent handwritten letters and I spent a week and a half responding to emails. People wanted us to know they still loved us and they still loved our son who had made a mistake; it meant so much.'

The report was still not out the day after the Tour finished, but I told the team I wanted to retire immediately and made my announcement via a media release. By this stage, I probably wasn't thinking clearly; it was a sudden decision but I didn't know how to retire from the sport and at the same time confess to what I had done fifteen years ago. Having already told Shayne and my family, I decided to confess publicly as well. With something this big, you don't just tell one person and that's it. Although the senate report wasn't out, by now I'd confessed to the people who meant the most to me, and nothing could have been worse than that.

A lot of people questioned 'Why now?' and claimed that it was only because of the French senate report, but that's easy for them to say. When you've achieved so much clean and on natural ability it's hard to confess to something that was done so long ago and that could taint everything. I fully admit that yes, it did take this last push and shove from the senate to make me realise that it was time to face up publicly to what I'd done and accept the consequences of my actions.

By the Wednesday when the senate report was due to be handed down I was back in Luxembourg. I didn't know where or when to look for it and was outside with my family when initial reports came through that I wasn't on the list. When that emerged, the obvious question I asked myself was, 'Okay, do I still go through with this?' I was almost upset that my name wasn't on the list because I was ready to talk and no story that any journalist could write would hurt more than me telling Shayne and my family. So I made up my mind that I would go through with it, regardless.

Eventually it came out that my name wasn't on a list of riders who tested positive at the 1998 Tour de France but on another list of those who were 'suspicious'. What the hell did that mean? What is suspicious? You could have a virus or be dehydrated and your blood samples could be up or down.

But there was no turning back. It was a pretty surreal moment and a day that I knew would change my life. I decided to text News Limited journalist Reece Homfray, who has helped me write this book, and tell him the truth.

I wanted to do it publicly then be around my family. As soon as we'd finished talking I turned off my phone. I'd said what I needed to say and that was it. There was no other story, no other angle; that's what happened and that was it.

There are no further admissions to lifelong or systematic doping and that's why I can be proud of my results and proud of my Olympic medals. The Olympics have got all my urine and blood tests stored away somewhere; they can test them for the next thousand years if they want.

I hugged my kids and got a lot of support from Anne-Marie. After a couple of days I turned my phone back on to find many messages from people saying, 'Times have changed, people make mistakes and remember what you've done for your sport.' But eventually it became impossible to walk past the computer at home and not check out the wider reaction to my confession.

What I read was hard to take. You can read a hundred messages of support but it only takes a couple of bad ones and your brain focuses on them. The hardest ones were comments about the Olympics and that I'd tainted my whole career. That's what cut me really deep.

I was removed from the Australian Olympic Committee's athletes' commission and other sporting organisations, but I completely understand that and I've written a letter of apology to president John Coates and other AOC members.

So much negativity came out. People were asking, 'Why didn't you say something earlier?' But what I was experiencing was the exact reason. When you do put up your hand, you're crucified, so who in their right mind would do that?

For a while it was like I was living two lives. Some days I felt like the worst person on the planet, but then my kids would run around the corner oblivious to what was happening, wanting to play because they'd barely seen me for a month. There were times I was quite depressed and this lasted for a few weeks. I'd look at a photo of me during my career and something that should have made me proud suddenly hurt because people now thought I had been cheating my whole career, which certainly wasn't the case.

Eventually it was time to look forward. Anne-Marie had been planning my fortieth birthday which should have been a time to celebrate. Initially I decided that I didn't want to see or talk to anyone, and we should call off the party. But when I stopped and realised that everyone who was invited had contributed something special to my life, and to the person I believe I am, I wanted to go ahead with it.

About sixty people, mostly from Europe, attended my birthday; it was a massive show of support. It was a really important opportunity to confront everything that had happened and to thank my guests for being there because every single person in that room had had a positive influence on my life, whether they were friends we'd met in Luxembourg or old teammates and coaches. It really did click me out of my depressed bubble and make me realise there are people who support Stuart O'Grady the person not Stuart O'Grady the bike-rider.

Bannan says Stuart's confession triggered a range of responses.

'There were many emotions that went through my mind. Obviously, the first one was real disappointment in the fact he'd made that decision at that particular time,' Bannan says. 'But there was also an understanding of the environment and imagining the pressures those guys were under. Then I thought about what Stuart and his family were going through. The biggest thing would have been standing in front of his family and telling them what had happened.'

Bannan says he did fear the repercussions of Stuart's confession on the team, which had conducted an independent review into the doping history of its riders and staff earlier in the year.

'I certainly thought, "How is this going to affect the team?" given we'd just been through the Nicki Vance review. Stuart had been interviewed by ASADA and had not been truthful. But at the end of the day, we are not the FBI or CIA; we rely on honesty and the information athletes give us, and in this particular case Stuart was untruthful and that's where the disappointment comes in. But also the understanding that none of us knows the pressures those guys were under, which is where the compassion comes into it.'

In Bannan's view, Stuart's doping in 1998 does not undo his lifetime of work. 'I knew Stuart before that period. His involvement with the national program and the last two years with GreenEDGE—his commitment and responsibility was 100 per cent first class. From that point of view he was certainly part of a solution not part of a problem.

'To be stripped of all recognition because of a mistake in 1998 would be unfair. What he went through once he came out with the admission was pretty tough, and I know Stuart has a lot of work to do to regain trust in people, which I feel he will do in time.'

Orica-GreenEDGE owner Gerry Ryan says despite what happened, this won't be the last the sport will see of Stuart. 'I look forward to Stuart returning to Australia and to a position in cycling as he has a lot to offer, especially to young cyclists. I'm sure Australian cycling will be in a better place with him being involved,' Ryan says.

***

Days went by, I looked at my bike and decided I wasn't ready to get back on. After so many years my bike had become a symbol of pain, suffering and hurting. Eventually I went for a couple of rides with Dad and Seth, and to have three generations riding along together woke me up again. Despite what had happened, riding with my dad and my son was one of the proudest moments of my life.

It also helped me realise that I still wanted cycling to be part of my future. Hopefully time will heal the hurt I've inflicted on myself and others, and while it's hard to see a bright, rosy future right now, I'm already thinking of ways I can help others and be of guidance. I can use my experiences to help people, and it may not just be cyclists, it could be people of all walks of life who find themselves facing difficult decisions.

I want my children to one day read this book and be proud of what I achieved rather than ashamed of a bad decision I made. I want to teach them that you have to go through life's good and bad experiences and, importantly, you have to learn from them.

In life, we're confronted with many choices. I didn't always make the correct decision, but if I can at least steer my children in the right direction and be there to support them, that's more important than anything I have ever accomplished on a bike.

My final message to you is: don't be afraid to aim high and don't be afraid to fail. You can be whatever you want in life. Every single person on this planet can achieve the most ambitious goals if they want it badly enough. Do you think Sir Donald Bradman, Dawn Fraser, Ron Barassi, Mick Doohan, Cathy Freeman, Greg Norman, Mat Rogers, Sir Hubert Opperman and so many more never faced challenges? People would have told them to stop dreaming.

It doesn't matter how tall you are, how much you weigh, what your background is or where you went to school. Go after your dream, and if you don't achieve it the first time, then try again. Get advice and listen to the people around you. Most importantly, respect all the people in your life, not only those who are above you. Respect is something that no amount of money in the world can buy, and it will last forever.

Be sure to play the game fair and square. Be true to yourself, to your values and what you know is right. Don't do anything you may later regret. Life is short, but it is also long and, as I've experienced the hard way, the truth always comes out.

Make the most of life and don't be afraid to go all-in. Failure should only make you even more determined. You could be that guy or girl screaming and clapping at the person in front of you. Or you could be the person standing on the field, the pitch, the velodrome or anywhere in the world, reaping the rewards of dedication, commitment and sacrifice.

I've always said that pain is temporary and memories are forever, so have a go.

PALMARES

1992
Silver, Team Pursuit, Barcelona Olympics

1993
Gold, Team Pursuit, World Championships, Vikingskipet

1994
Gold, Team Pursuit, Commonwealth Games, Victoria
Gold, Scratch Race, Commonwealth Games, Victoria
Silver, Points Race, Commonwealth Games, Victoria
Bronze, Individual Pursuit, Commonwealth Games, Victoria
Bronze, Team Pursuit, World Championships, Palermo

1995
Gold, Team Pursuit, World Championships, Bogota
Bronze, Individual Pursuit, World Championships, Bogota

1996
Bronze, Team Pursuit, Atlanta Olympics
Bronze, Points Race, Atlanta Olympics

1997
7th, Gent Wevelgem

1998

1st, Stage 14, Tour de France
2nd, Points Classification, Tour de France
Wore the Tour de France yellow jersey for three days
1st, Tour of Britain
Silver, time trial, Commonwealth Games, Kuala Lumpur
6th, Het Volk

1999

1st, Tour Down Under
2nd, Points Classification, Tour de France

2000

2nd, Tour Down Under
10th, Points Race, Sydney Olympics

2001

1st, Stage 5, Team Time Trial, Tour de France
2nd, Points Classification, Tour de France
Wore the Tour de France yellow jersey for six days
1st, Tour Down Under
2nd, GP de Villers–Cotterets

2002

Gold, Road Race, Commonwealth Games, Manchester
3rd, Points Classification, Tour de France
13th, Road Race, World Championships, Limburg
7th, Tour Down Under

2003

1st, Road Race, National Championships

1st, Centenary Classification, Tour de France

3rd, Tour of Flanders

3rd, Paris–Tours

3rd, Tour Down Under

2004

Gold, Madison, Athens Olympics

1st, Stage 5, Tour de France

4th, Points Classification, Tour de France

1st, Stage 5, Stage 7, Points Classification, Criterium du Dauphine

1st, HEW Cyclassics

3rd, Milan–San Remo

4th, Road Race, World Championships, Verona

1st GP de Villers–Cotterets

2005

2nd, Volta ao Algarve

2nd, Points Classification, Tour de France

3rd, Tour Down Under

4th, Milan–San Remo

10th, Gent–Wevelgem

2006

2nd, Grand Prix Zurich

3rd, Paris–Tours

6th, Road Race, World Championships, Salzburg

STUART O'GRADY

2007
1st, Paris–Roubaix
5th, Milan–San Remo
5th, Tour of California
4th, Milano–Torrino
10th, Tour of Flanders

2008
5th, Paris–Roubaix
8th, Gent–Wevelgem
10th, Tour Down Under
1st, Teams Classification, Tour de France

2009
2nd, Tour Down Under

2011
1st, Team Prologue, Stage 1, Vuelta a Espana,
10th, Milan–San Remo
9th, E3 Prijs Vlaanderen

2012
6th, Road Race, London Olympics
1st, Team Time Trial, Stage 1, Tirreno-Adriatico

2013
1st, Team Time Trial, Stage 4, Tour de France